FISHING FOR WEAKFISH

KEITH KAUFMAN

FISHING FOR WEAKFISH

KEITH KAUFMAN

THE FISHERMAN LIBRARY CORPORATION
1622 Beaver Dam Road
Point Pleasant, New Jersey 08742

PRINTED IN THE UNITED STATES OF AMERICA
Library of Congress Cataloging-in-Publication data
ISBN 0-923155-30-9

THE FISHERMAN LIBRARY CORP.
1622 Beaver Dam Road
Point Pleasant, New Jersey 08742

Publisher . . . . Richard S. Reina
Associate Publisher . . . . Pete Barrett
Copy Editor . . . . Linda Barrett
Cover Art. . . . . William Hopkins
Illustrations. . . . . Adrienne Kucharewski
Typesetting and Layout . . . . Typographic Solutions, Inc.

DEDICATION

To Uncle Bill and Uncle Harold. They took their eager young nephew fishing on New Jersey's bays and coastal waters, and on midwestern ponds and lakes. They taught me how to locate and catch fish, and how to have fun while doing it. But their gifts to me go far beyond catching fish. They instilled in me their deep appreciation of the outdoors and their respect of our wonderful natural resources. I have learned with them and laughed with them, even when we were wet and cold and the fish wouldn't bite. They talked with me, listened to me, shared their lives with me. And now, as I enjoy those same experiences with my two young sons, I appreciate even more just how fortunate I have been to fish with, and learn from, my Uncle Bill and Uncle Harold.

INTRODUCTION

In recent seasons there's been a significant and continual improvement in our weakfish and speckled trout action. Anglers from New England to Florida have been catching more fish, and more bigger fish, and loving every minute of it. Weaks and specks of 12 inches to 12 pounds have been caught. This indicates strong numbers of fish from several year classes, and provides evidence that intelligent fisheries management that effectively addresses the real issues and problems, and the implementation of realistic solutions, can and will rebuild our precious marine resources. We're on the verge of fantastic fishing for weaks and specks. Recreational and commercial fishermen have had to sacrifice to make this happen, but the reward is outstanding fishing, including plenty of trophy fish, the likes of which we haven't seen in nearly a generation.

During the late 1970s, weakfish of 7 to 10 pounds absolutely exploded upon the fishing scene! Weakfish of spectacular sizes were suddenly in great abundance. The late 1970s and early 1980s were the weakfish wonder years - even trophy tiderunners of 12 to 15 pounds were caught in good numbers! The fishing was fabulous from the mouth of Chesapeake Bay on up through New England. A common sight on the docks was two and even three anglers struggling to drag coolers bulging with weakfish of 8 pounds and up. It was the most awesome action that many of us had ever seen.

The sudden appearance of impressive weakfish was stunning because in the 1950s and 1960s weakfish had disappeared. Then somehow, some way, the few fish that were still around slowly began a comeback. By the early 1970s, weakfish had rebounded. I was a teenager then and I had a blast catching weakies with my Uncle Bill in Delaware Bay and Great Bay in New Jersey. They were 12 to 14 inchers, and fishermen along the Atlantic Coast were delighted to have them.

Then, huge weakfish - fish measured in pounds, not inches - showed up and changed everything. Tiderunner weakfish and anglers' passion for them put small, quiet towns like Milford, Delaware, and Fortescue, New Jersey, and dozens of others along the East Coast, on the map. The World Championship Weakfish Tournament was one of scores of tournaments spawned by the weakfish boom. Sponsored by the Southern Delaware Chamber of Commerce in Milford, this tournament could feature exciting prizes such as a free Grady-White boat and trips to Europe because fishermen from near and far eagerly plopped down their entry fees with high expectations of landing big fish and thrilling prizes. Big tiderunner seatrout of 9 to 14 pounds hit the scales in that tournament every year. On Saturdays and Sundays from May through August it was practically impossible to get seated, even at 5 a.m., in angler-packed restaurants in Lewes, Delaware, Cape May, New Jersey, and elsewhere. Charter boat captains had all of the business they could handle. They ran two, even three trips a day, seven days a week, all in pursuit of abundant tiderunners. Captains had to turn other anxious anglers away simply because their calendars were crammed full with upcoming trips. It seemed like it would never end, but sadly, we were to learn that weakfish were a limited, and precious resource.

Weakfish catches began to fall off in the mid 1980s. Many factors were responsible, including non-relenting recreational and commercial fishing pressure, a lack of sound fisheries management, power plants and the shrimp trawl industry that devastated juvenile weakfish by the tons, and the natural population cycles of the species. By the late 1980s and early 1990s it was all over - weakfish numbers had crashed. Not only did the World Championship Weakfish Tournament have to be discontinued due to a lack of fish, but the Southern Delaware Chamber of Commerce closed its doors for good when anglers quit coming to town.

But there's hope. There's been a resurgence; weakfish are again increasing in size and numbers. Careful management of the recreational and commercial weakfish harvest, and other factors, have enabled the weakfish stock to rebuild. We're well on our way to more fabulous action like that of the halcyon years of the 1970s and early 1980s! Twelve to 15-inch weakfish are still common catches, especially among summertime bottom bouncers. Yet recent springs and autumns have featured action with an ever-increasing number of 3 to 7-pound weakfish. And anglers with the experience and expertise to effectively fish jetties, lighthouses, bridges, wrecks and other structure, have been hooking up with more 7 to 12 pounders.

Speckled trout stocks have also been up and down over the years, yet there's encouraging news in that regard too. The Florida net ban and the remarkable rebound of speckled trout and other species are perhaps the brightest examples of how addressing the real problems with meaningful regulations and management practices can bring back fish populations that were nearing total collapse.

With proper diligence and management on our part, the weakfish and speckled trout recoveries will continue and strengthen. There's much to look forward to on the weakfish and speckled trout front during the beginning of this new millennium!

ACKNOWLEDGEMENTS

I thank Richard S. Reina, Vice President of *The Fisherman* magazine; Fred Golofaro, Publisher; and Associate Publisher Pete Barrett for providing me with two fantastic opportunities: To write this book, and to serve for 10 years as Managing Editor of *The Fisherman's* Mid Atlantic edition. I benefited greatly from the writing, editing, journalism and angling skills of Fred and Pete, and other *Fisherman* staffers including Tim Coleman (New England Edition Managing Editor), Tom Melton (Long Island Edition Managing Editor), and Dusty Rhodes (former New Jersey Edition Editor). I have learned much about fishing, and writing, from all of the writers and field editors of *The Fisherman,* and many of the magazine's readers and advertisers have made me a better writer by providing me with their input on fishing issues, hot spots, locations and techniques.

Joe Morris and I both came on board at *The Fisherman* on Labor Day of 1989. Joe's comprehensive fishing and boating expertise that he shared with me was a tremendous asset during our early days together in Lewes, Delaware. And, I recall that summer night at Brandywine Light when we had a blast bucktailing nice weakfish aboard Joe's boat Mojo.

Bill Hall and Pete Dressler are two incredibly talented anglers and fishing with them is always a valuable learning experience. They have demonstrated for me firsthand how to locate and catch big weakfish and speckled trout at Brandywine Light in Delaware Bay, The Cell and Sharps Island Light in Chesapeake Bay, the Chesapeake Bay Bridge Tunnel, and other Mid-Atlantic locations. Their techniques will catch weaks and specks anywhere, and they are included in this book.

I extend a note of appreciation to my 11th grade English teacher, Mr. Ed Appel. I can still vividly recall the enjoyment and excitement he brought to our studies of Moby Dick, Our Town, and the Gettysburg Address, and how they demonstrated the beauty and power of clear, concise, creative writing.

Abraham Lincoln said "Everything that I am, and ever hope to be, I owe to my dear mother". The same is true for me, except in my case my wife would also be included in that acknowledgement. I am forever grateful for the guidance, support, love and friendship that I have received from both my mother Evelyn, and wife Stephanie. I have shared a lifetime with my brother Bruce, and look forward to many more upcoming fishing adventures with him in the years to come.

My favorite fishing companions are my two young sons. The excitement and enthusiasm that Cody and Ross radiate during a day on the water bring an entire new level of enjoyment and reward to my fishing experiences. I have been very fortunate to fish with, work with, and be friends with some outstanding anglers and wonderful people, including (but not limited to) Robbie Sourbeer, Jeff Kirchoff, Bill Hamilton, Al Wright, and Ed and Connie Vallish.

TABLE OF CONTENTS

Chapter One

MEET THE WEAKFISH AND SPECKLED TROUT

Weakfish, seatrout, gray trout. Depending on where you live and fish, this fish of many monikers may also be known as yellowfin trout, weakies, tiderunners and squeteague. This incredibly beautiful and popular species is targeted by surf fishermen, bottom bouncers, casters, trollers and fly fishermen from New England to Florida. Their appeal also stretches far inland, as anglers from Pennsylvania, Ohio, West Virginia, Vermont and beyond gladly travel long distances at all hours of the day and night, and invest considerable amounts of time and money, all for the opportunity to pursue their favorite species in the Atlantic and its many bays, sounds and tributaries.

Weakfish provide fishing excitement all the way from Massachusetts south to Florida's East Coast. The greatest numbers of fish are caught each year from the mouth of Chesapeake Bay near Virginia Beach north to New York. Chesapeake Bay, Delaware Bay, coastal New Jersey and Peconic Bay on Long Island in New York usually feature the largest populations of weakfish.

A southern cousin of the weakfish, speckled trout are most abundant from the Gulf of Mexico and Florida to Chesapeake Bay. Some specks are caught each year in Delaware and New Jersey, and even as far north as New York; many of the speckled trout taken in more northern waters are often caught on lures and baits intended for weakfish. While they're targeted by many Maryland anglers, the popularity of speckled trout skyrockets among fishermen in Virginia, North Carolina, and South Carolina. Farther south in Georgia and Florida, and along the Gulf Coast in Alabama, Mississippi, Louisiana and Texas, speckled trout are the undisputed king of the inshore fishing scene.

A wide range of fishing techniques can be used to catch both weakfish and speckled trout from skinny water in back bays and tidal rivers, to jetties and piers, on out to deeper-water wrecks and reefs.

The Weakfish

Many factors are responsible for the widespread appeal of weakfish, one of which is their spectacular beauty. Weakfish, especially fish fresh from the water, glow with enough dazzling colors to make a peacock jealous. The belly and lower sides are silver and white, the fins mostly yellow. The upper body radiates with iridescent purple, blue, green, and yellow hues, all exquisitely highlighted with small black spots along the back and sides. The rather large mouth features an upper and lower jaw that are equipped with a pair of long, thin teeth that serve weakfish well when it comes to grabbing and holding its prey. Immediately behind that impressive dental work are other smaller teeth that also help to make escape all but impossible for fish and crustaceans that fall victim to a weakfish attack. While weakfish aren't the chompers and devastators that bluefish are, smart anglers keep their fingers well clear of those front fangs.

Weakfish are often easy for anglers to get at, and this availability at easily-accessed locations is another factor that makes them a highly-attractive and entertaining target for anglers of all ages, means and fishing skills. While in pursuit of their favorite foods, weakfish will prowl the surf and also move into bays and back bays, sounds, inlets, and tidal rivers and creeks. Many trophy fish, and limit catches, have been made by anglers leisurely standing on a pier soaking squid strips on the bottom with a rig that features only a hook and a sinker. Docks, bridges, beaches and inlets also provide anglers with easy access and inexpensive action with weakfish. But on the other hand, weakfish also frequent shoals, drop-offs, lighthouse rockpiles, wrecks and reefs, where in-depth boating and fishing skills are required to locate and catch them, providing challenges and personal satisfaction that many fishermen find very rewarding.

Spawning And Migration

While April to June is prime time for weakfish spawning, hatching and early larval development, they can occur as early as March and as late as October. Spawning in many locations is believed to take place in the early evening and at night primarily over mud and sand bottom. The principal spawning area is from Chesapeake Bay north to Montauk Island.

Life for most weakfish begins sometime from late April through June when hatching takes place in estuarine zones along the coast. Young-of-the-year weakfish in Chesapeake and Delaware bays move from high to low salinity areas throughout the summer, then return to high-salinity waters in the fall, and exit the tributaries in October, November and December. In North Carolina, weakfish are known to spawn in Pamlico Sound and in or near inlets. Farther south, along the South Carolina and Georgia Coasts, spawning occurs in deeper water in sounds and in near-shore coastal waters.

It's believed that weakfish spend winters along or near the Continental Shelf from about Chesapeake Bay south through North Carolina. In the spring (March and April), as the water warms and

Weakfish provide exciting inshore fishing opportunities for anglers from Florida to New England. They're most abundant from Virginia Beach to New York.

DISTRIBUTION OF NORTHERN WEAKFISH

DISTRIBUTION OF SPOTTED SEA TROUT

the amount of daylight during each day increases, weakfish begin to migrate inshore and northward. They enter bays and sounds where sexually mature fish will spawn. After spawning, it seems many of the larger weakfish take up residence on heavy deeper-water structure such as lighthouse rockpiles, wrecks and reefs, while smaller fish move to shoals, sloughs, channels and drop-offs. Each autumn (October and November), falling water temperatures and less daylight trigger weakfish to vacate inshore waters. For weakfish that have summered in the Virginia Beach area and south, it's primarily an offshore movement to the Continental Shelf. For weakfish in Maryland, Delaware, New Jersey and points north, it's a southerly migration and also an offshore movement. Then in the spring, the annual inshore movement and northward migration begins again.

Big weakfish are the first to hit our bays and sounds in the spring, and they're followed by smaller weakfish later in the spring and summer. In Delaware Bay and other locations, the early-run big weakfish first show up in March and April. While the water is too cold at that time for weakfish to take baits or lures, recreational anglers must endure reports of 8 to 12-pound tiderunners being taken in commercial nets. Only in mid to late May, or whenever the water temperature hits at least 52 degrees, and preferably 55 degrees, will

Spring is a prime time to find big weakfish in the bays and sounds, as they arrive before the smaller weakfish, which appear later in the spring and summer.

the weakfish bite begin for recreational fishermen. Spring and fall are prime times for weakfish action, especially for bigger fish. All season, but especially during the heat of summer, many of the most impressive weakfish catches are made early in the mornings, in the evenings, and during the darkness of night.

Scientific Classification

The scientific name for weakfish is *Cynoscion regalis,* and it's a colorful and attractive member of the drum family, *Sciaenidae.* Weakfish and its relatives create a drumming sound by vibrating their swim bladders. In weakfish it's a low and pleasant sound, and it often triggers yet another sound - squeals of delight from youngsters as they have their first close encounter with a weakfish. I have read that it's only the male weakfish that can create the drumming and croaking sounds, which may be especially important for attracting female fish for spawning.

The drum clan includes fish of all shapes and sizes, including Atlantic croaker (hardhead) that only rarely exceed 3 pounds, broad-shouldered behemoth black drum that frequently weigh in excess of 80 pounds, 5 to 50-pound red drum, and panfish-sized spot, king-fish and silver perch - which provide exciting and enjoyable fishing opportunities in their own right.

Speckled Trout

Many anglers claim that the remarkable beauty of spotted seatrout, also known as speckled trout and specks, surpasses that of even the elegantly colorful weakfish. The back and upper sides of a speckled trout are an attractive combination of gray and blue with a smidgen of green, while the lower sides and belly are a bright silver. The spots on speckled trout are larger and more pronounced than those on weakfish, and spots also decorate the yellowish-green tails, dorsal fins and caudal fins of speckled trout.

Speckled trout and weakfish are at times caught in the same areas and on the same type of structure, including the pilings and boulders of the Chesapeake Bay Bridge Tunnel in Virginia, on other Mid-Atlantic rockpiles, and in the North Carolina surf. However, generally speaking, anglers catch the most speckled trout in relatively shallow water in bays, sounds, tidal rivers and other backcountry areas, especially in locations featuring grassy bottoms. Grass and vegetation provide protection and feeding areas for speckled trout and also many of their favorite foods.

Spotted trout, also known as speckled trout or specks, are a close relative of the weakfish and frequent the shallow waters of bays, sounds and tidal rivers.

While its body shape closely resembles that of weakfish, speckled trout usually do not get as consistently large as weakfish, although trophy specks are taken each year. Many of the speckled trout caught by anglers are from 1 to 3 pounds. Southern anglers commonly refer to big 4 to 7-pound specks as "gator trout". Huge 8 to 10-pound speckled trout are considered to be true trophy fish. While still a somewhat rare catch, a few more speckled trout over 10 pounds have been caught in recent seasons. In 1999, Claude Bain, director the Virginia Saltwater Fishing Tournament, reported that 25 specks over 9 pounds, and 11 over 10 pounds, had been registered with the tournament. The largest speck taken in Virginia in 1999 was Harvey Caldwell's monster fish of 12 pounds, 3 ounces - the largest speckled trout taken in Virginia since 1981!

Feeding Habits

Weakfish have a wide and varied diet. Practically any fish that they can grab and swallow are fair game, including killifish, anchovies, silversides, spearing, butterfish, menhaden, eels, squid, spot, croaker, white perch, snapper bluefish, porgies, and even juvenile weakfish. Weakfish also crave crustaceans, including a variety of crabs, grass shrimp, mantis shrimp and sand fleas.

Pursuit of their favorite foods will bring weakfish to many different locations, each of which provides its own convenience or challenges to anglers. Weakies will move into very skinny water right up against the shore in back bays and tidal creeks to gulp down grass shrimp. Fishermen can enjoy light-tackle and fly fishing action while walking the shoreline and marsh banks, or even while wading. The best bite often comes early in the mornings and in the evenings, during the beginning of outgoing tide as the falling water will flush shrimp from the beaches and grasses. Lights on docks, piers and bridges attract small baitfish, which in turn bring in hungry weakfish, and this makes docks, piers and bridges ideal and easy fishing platforms, especially in low-light conditions. The surf and inlets are favorite locations for many anglers because they're often alive with the bait-fish and crabs that weakfish can't resist. Plus, weakfish will often fol-low more aggressive bluefish and stripers into inlets and the surf where the weakfish will feed on the scraps and injured bait created by their fellow predators. The rocky bases of lighthouses, and bay and ocean structure such as shoals, sloughs, wrecks, channels and shell-bottom areas are some of the other key weakfish spots to be examined in this book.

Weakfish possess voracious appetites and large mouths, and will feed on practically any other fish or prey species they can swallow.

Since weakfish chow down on many different types of fish and crabs, they can be taken on an immense variety of baits and lures. That includes everything from simple bucktails to metal jigs to some of today's flashy and colorful plugs and lures. Fishing tactics from bottom bouncing to trolling to flycasting can be used to produce limit catches of big weakfish.

Weakfish are predators, yet as members of the marine food chain they themselves also fall victim to predation. Little weakfish are eaten by big weakfish. Weakfish of various sizes are also very appetizing to bluefish, sharks, doormat fluke (summer flounder), stripers, cobia, amberjack and other inshore predators.

Speckled trout generally have a narrower diet than weakfish. Crabs and shrimp are among their favorites, and they're found in greatest abundance in relatively shallow grassy-bottom areas, usually in tidal rivers, sounds, bays and their tributaries. At these locations speckled trout are excellent sport for light-tackle live bait fishermen and lure casters, and also flyrodders. In Florida and elsewhere, specks provide particularly exciting shallow-water action for anglers who suspend live shrimp and other small live baits under a bobber and drift them over grass-beds where they're ambushed by speckled trout.

1980 - 1998 Average

AGE	L (In.)	W (lbs.)	Most Recent (1998) AGE	W (lbs.)
1	8.0	0.3	1	0.2
2	10.7	0.6	2	0.4
3	13.4	1.0	3	0.7
4	16.1	1.4	4	1.1
5	18.7	2.4	5	1.6
6	21.4	3.6		
7	24.1	6.7		
8	26.8	11.0		
9	29.5	11.2		
10	32.2	12.7		
11	34.9	13.0		
12	37.6	13.4		

Weight vs length chart

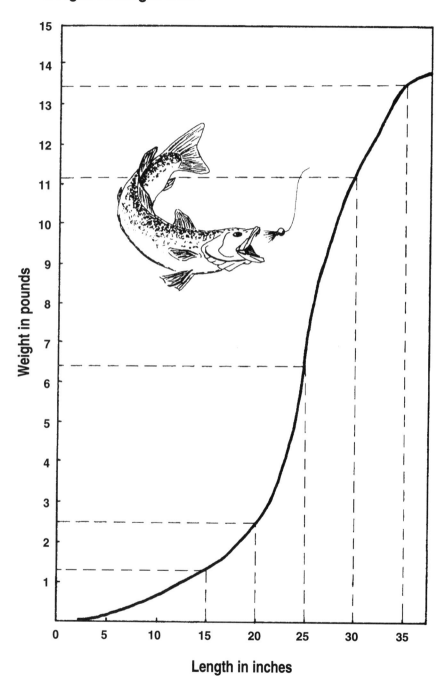

Speckled trout will often expand their dining choices beyond crabs and shrimp. Specks, especially bigger fish of 4 pounds and up, will also devour minnows, mullet, small menhaden and other baitfish. These baits, and also trophy specks, are found in the surf and on bridges, rockpiles and wrecks.

Management

In state waters, which are from the beach to three miles out, weakfish are managed by the Atlantic State Marine Fisheries Commission (ASMFC), and each particular coastal state's fish and game division. In federal waters from three to 200 miles offshore (the Exclusive Economic Zone or EEZ), weakfish are managed by the Fishery Management Councils of the United States Department of Commerce.

Weakfish have supported recreational and commercial fisheries along the Atlantic Coast since the early 19th century. Their economic importance was a major reason for the development of coastwide management plans by the ASMFC in 1985, 1992 and 1997. The recreational catch of weakfish is regulated by daily creel limits at a preferred minimum size of 12 inches. The commercial weakfish

Though the weakfish rebound that began in the mid and late 1990s is still underway, the outlook for the anglers of tomorrow looks promising with continued conservation.

fishery is regulated by a combination of seasonal closures, area closures, and mesh size regulations. To further conserve weakfish, the Management Plan also encourages the use of bycatch reduction devices for the shrimp fishery in the South Atlantic. Studies have indicated that Atlantic Coast weakfish should be managed as a single, interdependent unit.

Fishery data indicate that in terms of numbers of weakfish and the weight of those fish, most of the recreational catch is made from Virginia to New York. Fisheries officials also state that the proportion of weakfish released in the recreational fishery "has risen abruptly since 1990 to over 40% of the catch", mainly due to "implementation of higher minimum size limits (size limits from 12 to 16 inches), and lower creel limits". They also assume that 20% of the fish released alive eventually die. While it is generally recognized that weakfish are more susceptible to stress and injury than bluefish, stripers and some other inshore species, many in the recreational fishery dispute the 20% mortality figure on released weakfish as being much too high. That estimate of 20% seems especially obsolete when one considers the ever-increasing usage of circle hooks among recreational anglers, and the continuing efforts of conservation organizations to better educate anglers on how to carefully land, handle, unhook and release fish.

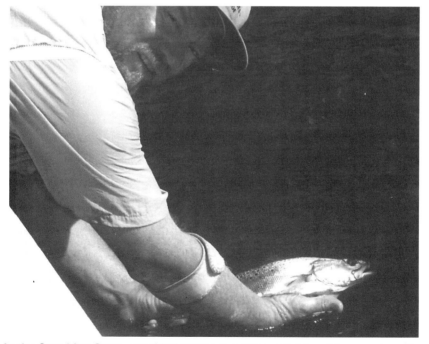

In the Sunshine State, speckled trout have rebounded in a big way since the implementation of the Florida net ban.

Annual commercial landings of weakfish have been highest in North Carolina, with most of the fish caught in gillnets. Weakfish are also taken commercially by otter trawls, pound nets and haul seines.

From 1982 to 1988, the recreational weakfish catch was described as "high and relatively stable" with catches of about 2,500 metric tons to 5,300 metric tons per year. After 1988, catches started to fall off considerably, and they plummeted to an all-time low of only 597 metric tons in 1993. On the commercial side, total weakfish landings from Massachusetts to Florida (1970 to 1996) peaked in 1980, with a commercial take of 16,312 metric tons. The weakfish collapse of the 1980s and 1990s hit bottom commercially in 1994 with a harvest of 2,873 metric tons.

However, the present and future are immensely brighter than the recent past as a rebound in weakfish numbers that began in the late 1990s has been treating recreational anglers to much-improved fishing, including greater numbers of bigger fish. Fisheries officials report above-average recruitment, plus there are indications that the age structure of weakfish is expanding. "Continued low fishing mortality rates and good recruitment should allow for extension of the age structure to a point comparable to that observed in the early 1980s."

While fisheries managers often burden recreational anglers with severe size and creel limits in their attempts to restore fish stocks, the evidence clearly shows that in many cases it's wasteful commercial practices that are often responsible for the decimation of certain species. Pete Barrett, Associate Publisher of *The Fisherman* magazine, made an excellent point in the magazine's New Jersey Edition when he wrote that much of the credit for the weakfish comeback goes to the North Carolina Marine Fisheries Commission. The Commission instituted a 10-inch minimum size on weakfish (vigorously opposed by commercial watermen), banned the use of flynets south of Cape Hatteras (vigorously opposed by commercials), and fought hard to stop the loss of undersized weakfish in shrimp trawls (vigorously opposed by commercials). The state of North Carolina took the steps necessary to prevent the enormous, indiscriminate slaughter of juvenile weakfish and allowed these fish to reach spawning age. Barrett correctly stated that the coast-wide recreational catch barely took a hit as weakfish were so low in population that anglers simply weren't catching big numbers of them despite the changes in bag and size limits that were instituted. Once the wasteful practices were stopped, the weakfish population soared. This recovery did not happen with draconian recreational reductions in an attempt to be "fair" to both sides. The slaughter of juvenile weakfish was clearly identified as a commercially-caused problem, and the resolution of the problem applied proper restrictions to prevent the destruction of juvenile fish. The result is a resurgence of weakfish that has enabled both commercials and recreationals to now experi-

Much of the credit for the weakfish comeback goes to the North Carolina Marine Fisheries Commission, which worked to end the indiscriminate commercial slaughter of juvenile weakfish.

27

ence good weakfish action.

Speckled trout in Florida provide another great example of how fish stocks can be increased when the real problems are identified and corrected. Thanks to the remarkable efforts of Karl Wickstrom and everyone at *Florida Sportsman* magazine, plus the residents of the Sunshine State, most commercial nets were banned from inshore waters in the early 1990s. While the net ban was vehemently (and at times violently) opposed by commercial fishermen, the results have been nothing short of spectacular. According to Captain Rick Grassett at Snook Fin-Addict Charters in Sarasota, Florida, a number of species are larger and more plentiful than they were before the ban, including speckled trout, redfish, jack crevalle and ladyfish. Plus, Captain Rick says there has also been "real big increases in fish that were once more of an incidental catch." Permit and pompano, which had been preciously few and far between in Sarasota and other areas of Florida, are now available in good numbers. Captain Merrily Dunn at Game Fish-Her Charters in Sarasota reports yet another benefit of the Florida net ban. She said eliminating the commotion of nighttime netting on the flats has made speckled trout and other species much more responsive to lures and flies.

Record Book Catches

A check of the International Game Fish Association (IGFA) record book shows that Jones Beach Inlet and Fire Island in New York, Delaware Bay in Delaware and New Jersey, and Chesapeake Bay in Virginia, have produced a number of IGFA weakfish record catches. And not surprisingly, a vast majority of record-setting weakfish were caught during the 1980s when big tiderunners were abundant.

There is a two-way tie, at 19 pounds, 2 ounces, for the IGFA All-Tackle Record weakfish. Dennis R. Rooney caught his impressive weakfish on October 11, 1984, at Jones Beach Inlet on Long Island, New York. Astonishingly, Rooney's remarkable catch was made with 8-pound test line! On May 20, 1989, William E. Thomas landed in the IGFA record books when he hooked, battled and boated a huge 19-pound, 2-ounce Delaware Bay weakfish. That immense fish was captured on 12-pound test line.

The IGFA record book also shows that some rather hefty weakfish have been subdued on relatively skinny line. The record holder in the 6-pound line category is Joseph Giallanzo with a big 17-pound, 8-ounce weakfish caught at Fire Island Inlet in New York in 1976. The 4-pound line weakfish record is a 14-pound, 5-ounce fish caught at Cape May, New Jersey, by Matthew D. Welsh in 1986. Ellyson S. Robinson III holds the top spot in the 2-pound line category with an 11-pound, 12-ounce weakfish caught in Chesapeake Bay in Virginia in 1982.

Fly fishermen have also made the IGFA record books with impressive weakfish catches. Norman W. Bartlett established the 4-pound tippet weakfish record with a jumbo 14-pound, 2-ounce weakie caught in Delaware Bay on June 5, 1987. The 6-pound tippet record is a 10-pound, 4-ounce weakish Gary L. Rudy caught in Cape May Court House, New Jersey, in 1980. A 10-pound, 11-ounce tiderunner, caught by Lawrence E. Haack in Chesapeake Bay in Virginia in 1983, is the 12-pound tippet record holder. The top weakfish in the 16-pound tippet category is an 11-pound, 2-ounce trophy catch caught by Howard F. Guja at Lloyd Point in New York in 1985, while the 20-pound tippet record was claimed by Art Greason on May 6, 1999, with a 10-pound, 1-ounce weakfish taken at Virginia Beach in Virginia.

The All-Tackle record holder among women is June Andrejko with a big 17-pound, 14-ounce weakfish caught on 16-pound line at Fayerweather Island, Connecticut, on September 13, 1986. Other women weakfish records listed in the IGFA record book include a 16-pound, 1-ounce fish Carole Mysliborski caught on 20-pound test at Southold Bay at Greenport, New York, on May 24, 1990; a 15-pound, 9-ounce weakfish captured on 30-pound line at Fire Island, New York, on May 18, 1986, by Joy E. Librizzi Bonvino; and a 14-pound, 11-ounce Delaware Bay weakfish caught by Cheri Wallace

The vast majority of record-setting weakfish were caught in the 1980s when big fish were more abundant.

at Cape May, New Jersey, on 12-pound line, on June 1, 1989.

Every speckled trout in the IGFA record book has come from one of two southern states: Florida and Texas. The IGFA All-Tackle Record was established on May 11, 1995, when Craig F. Carson weighed in an absolutely huge 17-pound, 7-ounce speckled trout that he had caught on 20-pound line at Fort Pierce, Florida. Other spectacular speckled trout catches that have landed in the IGFA record book include the 30-pound line category record holder, a monstrous 15-pound, 6-ounce speck, captured by Michael J. Forenny at Jensen Beach, Florida, in 1969. The women's All-Tackle Record, at an impressive 14-pounds, 6-ounces, belongs to Viola J. Hernandez III with the big fish she caught on 8-pound class line at Texas City Flats in Texas on November 17, 1984. She also holds the 2-pound line women's record with a 9-pound, 10-ounce speckled trout also caught at Texas City Flats. Barbara Smith Arthur has her name in the IGFA record book three times as she holds the women's 12-pound line record with a 12-pound, 2-ounce speck, the 16-pound line record with an 11-pound, 11-ounce fish, and the 4-pound line category record with a 10-pound, 6-ounce speck. All three of those dandy speckled trout were caught at Melbourne Beach in Florida.

Among speckled trout fly fishermen, the IGFA 16-pound tippet record holder is Sidney A. Friefeld with a 12-pound, 7-ounce speckled trout pulled from Indian River in Sebastian, Florida, on March 5, 1984. Dave Chermanski holds both the 6-pound tippet record (8-pound, 12-ounce speck), and the 8-pound tippet record (11-pounds, 8-ounces), with big fish hauled from the Banana River in Florida. The 2-pound tippet record has been held by Chuck Scates with an 8-pound, 11-ounce spotted seatrout caught at South Padre Island, Texas, in 1989.

Women fly fishermen looking to get their names in the IGFA record book have plenty of opportunities to do so as the following tippet classes for both weakfish and speckled trout are vacant: 2-pound, 4-pound, 6-pound, 8-pound, 12-pound and 16-pound. In fact, the only lady fly rod record holder is Wanda S. Morgan with a 7-pound, 11-ounce weakfish she caught on 20-pound tippet in West Ocean City, Maryland, on May 25, 1998. The 20-pound tippet category for speckled trout is vacant.

The IGFA keeps records of fish caught in many pound-test categories, for men and women, on standard tackle and fly tackle, in saltwater and freshwater. The IGFA also works hard to protect fish and our valuable marine resources from over-fishing and other destructive practices. Membership in IGFA is available for $25 per year and members receive the following: the bi-monthly *International Angler* magazine; discount fares with participating charter captains, hotels, lodges and resorts; IGFA decals and embroidered patches; and the annual *World Record Game Fishes* publication.

Learn more by visiting the IGFA website at WWW.IGFA.ORG. The email address is IGFAHQ@aol.com. The phone number is 954.927.2628, while the fax is 954.924.4299. Or write: International Game Fish Association, 300 Gulf Stream Way, Dania Beach, FL 33004.

Chapter Two

TACKLE AND EQUIPMENT

What incredible technological advancements we have witnessed in the fishing tackle industry! In the late 1970s, graphite provided us with a light-weight and extremely sensitive material that is now commonly used in the construction of rods and reels. Lightweight graphite rods and reels provide casting comfort and accuracy, their enhanced sensitivity makes it much easier to detect strikes, plus graphite packs the power to administer hard hooksets and win tough battles with strong fish. Now some rods and reels–Fenwick AV reels for example–contain Aramid Veil fibers, the very same lightweight, rugged materials used to make bulletproof vests!

Additional ball bearings, centrifugal braking systems, improved drag systems, baitrunner features and other developments have dramatically enhanced the ease of operation and increased angler success with spinning, baitcasting and conventional reels. The baitrunner feature on some spinning reels makes them very effective when fishing live bait for weaks and specks, a fishing method that prior to baitrunner features was very cumbersome with spinning reels. Baitcasting reels are now much more fishermen-friendly. Their use among boating and surfcasting anglers continues to soar, thanks in large part to precision anti-backlash features such as centrifugal braking systems. They make these reels more forgiving–the slightest slip of the thumb does not necessarily result in a maddening backlash that resembles a bird's nest made of mono.

For years, the choice of which line to use was rather straightforward. For casting, there were lines that were smooth and supple. They provided casting distance and accuracy, yet they were usually a little lacking when it came to strength and abrasion resistance. Tougher lines were available when strength and durability were needed, but they were relatively rigid and featured lots of memory that made them difficult to cast with any accuracy or distance. But now line manufacturers use modern technology to combine the best of all worlds. We have high-tech lines that are soft and limp for the pinpoint casting of plugs and bucktails, yet they're also rugged enough to fight abrasion from wrecks and rockpiles. Other improvements in fishing line made possible by advancements in research, chemical engineering and manufacturing techniques include low-visibility lines for more strikes, low-stretch lines for better strike detection and stronger hooksets, and thinner-diameter lines for greater casting distance and less water resistance.

Superbraided lines, including Berkley Fire Line, JWA's SpiderWire Braid and SpiderWire Fusion, Bass Pro Shops Excel Nitro, and Western Filament T.U.F. lines - to name a few - have come

With the proper tackle it's possible to subdue even the largest weakfish.

Light-tackle fishermen enjoy the challenges and excitement that big weakfish provide.

on strong in recent seasons. These incredibly tough lines feature a thinner diameter than monofilament of comparable strength, providing for longer and accurate casts and less water resistance.

The resurgence of weakfish and speckled trout (also striped bass) has prompted many tackle manufacturers to develop and introduce specialized rods and reels, especially for shrimping and back bay fishing. There's lots of new tackle that is rather expensive, including inshore spinning and baitcasting reels that run $200 to $400 each. But a strong economy, great fishing action, and the tackle's superior performance and durability makes those expenditures well worth it for many anglers.

Rod, reel and line choices are many, and it's completely up to each individual angler to determine which they feel most comfortable with and most effective with in each fishing situation. While there are no "right" or "wrong" rods, reels or line to use, some will provide definite advantages in specific situations and will make fishing more enjoyable and successful. On the other hand, some tackle in certain situations will fatigue the angler, frustrate the angler and make it next to impossible for the angler to succeed. The following information should be used only as a guideline when it comes to rod, reel and line selection, which is strictly a matter of personal preference. Nothing beats time on the water and fishing experience in deciding which rod, reel and line feels right and performs right for you in your different fishing situations.

Reels

Because of the versatility, casting accuracy, comfort, convenience and sport that they provide, spinning reels are a favorite of weakfish and speckled trout fishermen far and wide. Anglers in boats, and on beaches, bridges, docks, piers and jetties use spinning tackle to fish artificial lures everywhere that these fish feed. Weakfish anglers arm themselves with spinning tackle when casting bucktails, leadheads with plastics, and plugs to weakfish on lighthouse rocks, bridge pilings, marsh banks, jetties, and bars and sloughs in the surf. Speckled trout anglers use spinning tackle to work MirrOlures in the surf and around mangrove roots, to fish speck rigs from boats and piers, and to pop shrimp suspended under a float over submerged grass-beds.

Previously, spinning reels weren't well suited for fishing live baits. The bails on spinning reels had to frequently be opened and closed to give line and then bring the rig under control, making spinning reels difficult to use and much less effective than conventional tackle. But that has changed in recent years with the development of baitrunner spinning reels. After casting out and activating the baitrunner feature, the reel will freely give line to slight pressure, which allows a live bait to swim naturally. It also makes it possible for a fish to grab the bait and swim with it without detecting any resistance. Then the angler deactivates the baitrunner by flipping the lever, and sets the hook. The versatility of spinning reels was even further enhanced and now they're used to put live spot, croaker, mullet and peanut bunker right in front of weaks and specks.

When it comes to casting lures, spinning reels generally provide the greatest casting distance, while baitcasting reels enable anglers to cast with precise accuracy. However, ease of operation has traditionally made spinning reels more of an angler favorite over baitcasting reels. After only a couple of hours of practice, even novices and children can cast a spinning reel with a fair degree of distance and accuracy. There is plenty of room for error, and mistakes are relatively easy to remedy. Not so with baitcasters. They are more difficult to cast than spinning reels, they are easier to backlash and tangle, and the tangles are often all but impossible to pull out - the line usually has to be cut and replaced. Considerable practice - days, weeks, even months - is required before an "educated thumb" is developed that can precisely control the spool and prevent frustrat-

Proper maintenance of all tackle, including rods, reels and rigs, is crucial to ensure everything goes smoothly when a weakie jumps on the other end of the line.

ing backlashes during casting. The time and effort invested in learning to fish a baitcasting reel are rewarded with pinpoint casting accuracy and a new level of fishing expertise and success. As previously mentioned, high-tech centrifugal braking systems and other recent anti-backlash developments have resulted in a significant reduction in learning time and a tremendous increase in the ease of operation and success that come with fishing baitcasting tackle. An example is Quantum's ACS external centrifugal brake control adjustment on its levelwind baitcasting reels that enable casters to dial in the amount of braking control they need simply by moving a click dial on the left side plate. Baitcasting reels by Daiwa, Shimano, Penn, Marado, Abu-Garcia and other manufacturers have casting controls that can all be very helpful when trying to achieve casting distance without backlashes.

The gear ratios and retrieve speeds of various reels must be considered when choosing reels for catching weaks and specks. Many of today's spinning reels feature high gear ratios and faster retrieve speeds. They can be used to effectively cast and swim plugs around jetties, lighthouse rocks and in the surf. However, the high gear ratios of spinning reels make it difficult to fish bucktails and leadheads low and slow on the bottom. The angler must turn the reel handle very s-l-o-w-l-y to keep the bucktail down deep. On the other hand, baitcasting reels and their lower gear ratios and slower retrieve speeds make it much easier to slowly bounce a bucktail across the bottom. The bait can be kept on or near the bottom without the agonizingly slow retrieve that is often required with spinning reels.

Many spinning and baitcasting reels on the market today feature quality construction and high-tech features. While some reels can be a little expensive, they perform incredibly well and with the proper care and maintenance they'll be dependable fishing companions for years, even decades.

Things to look for in a reel include a drag that smoothly gives up line to pressure - a spool that even slightly sticks or jumps could very well result in a broken line when a hooked trophy fish takes off on a strong run. The Abu Garcia CD series center drag reels with extra-large washers for a smooth, powerful drag, are but one example of the many advancements made recently in the design and performance of drags. Check the line guide on the bail of a spinning reel to ensure that it turns smoothly. Generally speaking, the more ball bearings a reel has the more smoothly and efficiently it will operate. For weakfish and speckled trout, look for reels that can hold at least 200 yards of 12 to 15-pound test line.

Pulling a bucktail, plug or spoon through the water puts a considerable strain on the line and reel, and it takes a tough and well-maintained reel to withstand the abuse that comes with trolling. Don't skimp and attempt to save a few bucks by purchasing inexpensive reels that will see a lot of trolling action, as the performance and durability of a quality conventional reel will make it well worth the extra cost.

When trolling shallow bays to search out concentrations of fish, many anglers use reels similar in size and line capacity to a Penn 310 GTi that are spooled with monofilament of about 17-pound test. In deeper-water trolling, superbraided lines and wire line often get the nod over monofilament because they make it easier to get lures down deep. Braided lines are thinner in diameter than mono, and superbraided and wire lines do not stretch. These characteristics enable these lines to better cut through the water and reach the bottom. To further ensure their lures remain on the bottom where big weakfish and speckled trout feed, many trollers with superbraided lines rig up with in-line sinkers (drails), while wire liners use a three-way swivel rig which holds a sinker that can weigh as much as 20 ounces. This heavy-duty trolling calls for a robust quality reel along the lines of a Penn 320 GTi.

Whether or not a levelwind on a trolling reel is a desirable feature is really a matter of personal preference. The 310 GTi and 320 GTi are both equipped with levelwinds, however, I also troll with a Penn 535 that does not have a levelwind. Without a levelwind, it's up to

Conventional and baitcasting reels enable anglers to fish bucktails and jigs low and slow on the bottom in the weakfish strike zone.

the angler to use their thumb to evenly distribute the line on the spool as the line is reeled in. A reel is spooled with wire line only after the reel is first loaded with at least 250 yards of 30-pound monofilament backing. After the mono backing is on the reel, then attach the wire line via an Albright Special or Uni-Knot, then reel from 150 to 250 feet of wire onto the spool.

Many of the same reels for trolling are used when livelining because big baits will attract large, powerful weakfish and speckled trout. Livelining is done with monofilament, not wire line. Along with the Penn 310 GTi, I have also fished live baits for years with my long-time favorite Penn Peer 209. The thumb is used to conveniently control the disengaged spool - when a fish grabs the bait the thumb is immediately lifted so line will freely come off the reel as the fish is allowed to briefly move off with the bait without detecting any resistance. After giving the fish enough time to get the bait fully in its mouth, engage the spool by flipping the lever, reel in all slack, and set the hook hard.

Jigging is simple and incredibly productive and I enjoy tremendously the action and fun that come with jigging for weaks and specks and many other inshore species. A small conventional reel or bait-casting reel is the top choice for jigging as it provides the line control

With conventional and baitcasting reels, anglers can control the line by simply applying pressure to the spool with their thumb. These reels are commonly used when bottom fishing with bait rigs, jigging and live-lining.

needed to keep the jig on the bottom and in the fish strike zone. My personal favorites include Pinnacle's Coastal CR 30, the Abu Garcia Ambassadeur 550 Plus, my old, yet reliable Penn Peerless No. 9, and the Abu Garcia Black Max 5600 or Black Max 6600W. The free-spool lever is flipped or the free-spool button is pushed to disengage the spool so the spoon or jig can sink to the bottom. Then the reel is re-engaged into gear, then the jigging process of raising and lowering the rod tip begins. When contact with the bottom is lost, the angler simply flips the lever or pushes the button on the reel to let out more line. When contact with the bottom is re-established, resume the jigging process. This is easy with conventional or baitcasting reels, but with spinning reels it can be a bit cumbersome to keep opening and closing the bail to let out more line.

Rods

While lightweight, sensitive graphite has become tremendously popular among rod manufacturers and fishermen, graphite and other new high-tech materials haven't completely replaced fiberglass in rod making, as fiberglass still offers appealing advantages of its own: it's

Despite the popularity of graphite rods today, fiberglass rods are still a durable and inexpensive option for weakfish anglers.

very durable and stands up well to abuse, plus fiberglass rods are often easier on the wallet than graphite and other high-tech rods.

But make no mistake about it, graphite helped trigger serious scientific advancements in rod making that continue to this day. Common now are terms such as HMF for "high modulus fibers". There are rods with 33 million modulus graphite, and 50 million modulus fibers, and 70 million modulus graphite construction, and so on. These refer to the modules of graphite used in the construction of a particular rod, and the more graphite modules used the more lightweight and sensitive the rod will be.

Cape Fear produces light-tackle spinning, casting and flycasting rods that are hexagonal in shape. The advantages include increased strength in a rod that's still very light weight and sensitive. The interior "I" beams of these rods are said to be nearly indestructible.

Years ago, before graphite rods, many weakfish and speckled trout anglers preferred slow-action rods that featured plenty of sweep in the tips. The general belief was that many fish were lost with stiff rods as the hook would tear free from the soft tissue of a weakfish or speckled trout mouth when the fish made a strong run. Limber rods with lots of sweep enabled the fish to run without applying too much pressure to the hook and pulling it out. However, the drawbacks of slow-action rods are a lack of sensitivity as strikes are not transmitted well through soft rods, and the difficulty in delivering a good, strong hookset with a rod that has lots of bend to it. In recent years, many anglers have shown a definite preference for fast-action graphite rods that have little sweep and provide for powerful hooksets, plus their sensitivity makes it easy to detect even the softest of strikes.

Graphite was a catalyst for more rod-building innovations. For example, Fenwick wraps some of its graphite rods with Aramid Veil, the material used in bullet-proof vests, to give the rods more impact resistance. To make its rods stronger and even more sensitive, Star Rods developed Nickelite, a process in which graphite impregnated with nickel is wrapped around a high-modulus graphite core. The list of rod-making advancements goes on and on.

Chemical engineers, scientists and tackle experts constantly examine the materials used to build rods, look for ways to improve construction techniques, and study the precise placement of guides, reel seats and handles. Rod manufacturers put forth this time, material and manpower to improve our fishing and attract new customers by developing rods packing the ultimate in fish-fighting power, casting accuracy, responsiveness, strength, balance and sensitivity.

In the mid 1990s I was a copywriter in the advertising and catalog department for Bass Pro Shops in Springfield, Missouri. To write the most accurate and effective advertisements about their tackle, I had no choice but to be very hands-on - it was my professional duty to study it and use it. That's when I first became familiar with Bass Pro Shops Graphite Series Rods, and now I wouldn't think of going weakfish jigging without them on board my boat.

My particular favorite is a 6-foot, 3-inch graphite rod, that's labeled a "Muskie" rod. The rod's action is listed as extra heavy, and it's rated for line of 14 to 40-pound test and lure weights of 5/8-ounce to 4 ounces. It's very affordably priced. Yet most important of all, it has the features that bottom bouncers should look for in all jigging rods, regardless of where the rod is purchased or who manufacturers it. The composite graphite rod construction, graphite reel seat and trigger handle provide the sensitivity needed to detect when a weakfish has inhaled a jig, and the strength to set the hook on big weakfish down deep. The aluminum oxide guides have also stood up well and have not been grooved by the superbraided lines I use for jigging. I have also used these same rods to fish bait on the bottom for fluke, drift eels for stripers, and to fish crab chunks on shallow wrecks and rocks for blackfish (tautog). At 6-feet, 3-inches, this type of rod can be comfortably handled and fished by my two young sons.

I no longer get paid to sell Bass Pro Shops rods, and I'm not push-

Many weakfish anglers still prefer slow-action rods for weakfish and speck-led trout to reduce the chances of pulling a hook from the fish's soft mouth.

ing their rods. Instead, I'm sharing with you what I have found to be beneficial features provided by these rods when used for jigging. Other similar rods by other manufacturers will perform just as well.

The rods typically used by weakfish trollers are 6-1/2 to 7-1/2 feet long and designed specifically for trolling. They feature the backbone and strength to handle the wire and superbraided lines, plus heavy sinkers, commonly used to get lures down deep. Hefty stripers and bluefish also inhabit the same structure where most weakfish trolling is done, and the rods need to be beefy enough to battle and subdue these big fish. Trollers using wire line and superbraided lines to pull bucktails, spoons and plugs along the bottom need to pay particular attention to the rod's guides. Over time, stainless steel or ceramic guides will groove as the wire or superbraided line actually cuts into the guide. It's important to use trolling rods featuring carboloy guides or aluminum oxide guides which are tough enough not to be damaged by wire or superbraided lines. Roller guides made by Fuji and Aftco also work well with wire line.

Boating anglers typically use 7-foot medium-action graphite spinning rods and 12 to 15-pound test monofilament or superbraided line when tossing plugs, bucktails and speck rigs to weakfish and speckled trout. When using superbraided lines with graphite rods it's important that care is taken to avoid broken rods. Take it from someone who has learned this the hard way. Unlike monofilament, superbraided lines do not stretch, and the rod absorbs a lot of the shock that comes with battling and boating hard-charging and flopping fish. Once, while my sons and I were having a blast catching breaking bluefish of 3 to 5 pounds on bucktails, I got in a hurry and laid a hooked bluefish on the motor box in my boat and attempted to unhook it while the rod was braced under my arm and held in an upright position (rod butt on deck of boat, rod tip pointing up). The bluefish flopped, slipped through my hands and slid off the motor box. The still-hooked blue fell toward the deck of the boat, and then suddenly it ran out of slack line, like a bungee-jumper. But instead of stretching the line and flexing the rod as would have happened with monofilament, the sharp impact of the bluefish coming tight on the unforgiving superbraided line created a sharp impact that shattered about the last six inches of a nice Penn graphite rod. It was a simple mistake, and it only took an instant, but it taught me a valuable lesson in attentiveness and care when fishing superbraids on graphite rods.

Surf fishermen looking for greater casting distance with plugs, bucktails and spoons hit the beaches with rods of eight feet to 9-1/2 feet in length. Graphite rods load and unload very quickly for longer casts and provide the sensitivity needed to detect strikes that come when the lure is still well off the beach. Jetty fishermen usually use slightly shorter rods of about seven feet in length because casting distance is not as crucial for them as it is surfcasters. In fact, jetty fishermen often cast at angles that enable them to work lures along (nearly parallel to) the rockpiles where weakfish and speckled trout feed. Penn, Daiwa, Berkley, Fenwick, St. Croix, Lamiglas and others make excellent spinning rods for casting lures from boats, beaches and jetties.

Beefier rods constructed of a composite of graphite and fiberglass are often used by surfcasters to heave bait rigs with heavier sinkers for long distances. These long and stout eight to 10-foot rods would be very expensive if constructed of just graphite, plus sensitivity is not as important when fishing bait rigs on the bottom.

Rods of 6-1/2 to seven feet are common among party boat anglers where rod strength, and the ability to control the rod and swing fish aboard in often crowded conditions, are more important than casting distance. Party boat rods also must possess the backbone needed to haul big weakfish up from the depths. The 6 foot, 3 inch "Muskie" rod in the Bass Pro Shops Graphite Rod Series that was mentioned earlier, and rods similar to it, are excellent choices for party boat fishing.

We've mentioned guides several times in describing the rods recommended for various fishing situations, and guides are something that should not be overlooked when it comes to rod selection. Fuji and other manufacturers make great efforts to develop guides that provide for greater casting distance, improved weight balance, and

Graphite rods are lightweight for casting and fishing comfort, and their sensitivity makes it easy to detect strikes when fishing with soft plastic baits.

more sensitivity, hooksetting power and reduced line twist. The major benefit of stainless steel guides is toughness, and they work well on party boat rods and jigging rods. As line is constantly let out or cast, and reeled in, and reeled in under the pressure of strong hooked fish, the line moves back and forth over the guides. This can eventually weaken the line. Ceramic and oxide guides reduce line wear, they do a good job of dissipating line-damaging heat caused by the friction of the line moving over the guides, and on spinning and baitcasting rods they provide for good casting distance. Yet they're not as durable as stainless steel guides.

A rod's reel seat, grip and butt are other factors to consider when choosing rods. Graphite reel seats on spinning and baitcasting rods provide outstanding sensitivity. Most rod grips and butts are made of either EVA foam or cork. They're both comfortable. After several years of use and exposure to the elements, foam can dry out and start to fall apart, while cork will chip more readily than foam. Many anglers who favor cork will tell you they appreciate the sensitivity it provides because it transmits even the slightest vibrations of strikes from the rod to the angler's hand.

Then there is always the long, on-going battle among some anglers over store-bought rods versus custom-made rods, one-piece rods versus two-piece rods. St. Croix, Fenwick, Penn, Berkley, Daiwa, Lamiglas and many other manufacturers provide us with excellent rods that excel when used in the situations they were designed for. They feature superior construction that's often loaded with quality features and these rods are available in tackle shops and fishing tackle catalogs at prices that range from very affordable to expensive. Many, many anglers have received years of excellent service from these rods. On the other hand, some more experienced anglers say custom-made rods are the only way to go. While more expensive, these fishermen appreciate the superb performance that comes with rods designed and constructed specifically with the angler's size, casting techniques and favorite fishing methods in mind. Many custom-rod anglers and other fishermen will use only one-piece rods, as they say a rod's performance and action are always diminished, even if only minimally, at the point where two-piece rods are joined together. Others use two-piece rods and appreciate the convenience they provide when it comes to transporting and storing them.

Building your own rod is yet another alternative. Many anglers pass the long, cold days of winter at their workbench, handcrafting rods that contain the specific features and qualities they desire in a rod. They enjoy the outstanding performance and the rewarding personal satisfaction that come with catching fish on rods they personally designed and constructed. Rod building courses are offered at many tackle shops and community colleges in coastal cities and communities.

Line And Leader

Fishing line is too often overlooked and under appreciated. That's unfortunate, because line is an extremely important component in our tackle and gear. It is our direct connection to the fish we hook and catch, and it's often responsible for many of the fish that are hooked and lost. Expensive rods and high-performance reels will be of little benefit when a big, strong fish applies pressure and snaps cheap, poor-quality fishing line, or line that should have been replaced long ago because it is frayed, nicked or aged. Many trophy fish are hooked each and every season only to be lost because the line had not received the attention and care it deserved.

Mistake number one is that fishing line isn't changed often enough. No monofilament fishing line should ever be used for more than one season. Never. When a hooked fish makes a mad dash for structure or the open ocean is no time to wish that you had spooled up with new line. Always replace line on every reel at the beginning of each new season - no questions asked. In fact, line should probably be replaced several times during the course of a single season, especially if you fish more than once or twice a week. Simply take

A wide variety of lines may be used to pursue weakfish, including monofilament, super braids and fluorocarbon.

off the old line, tie on new, fresh line, and carefully spool it on the reel so it goes on evenly and without twisting. There is no excuse whatsoever for risking the potential agony of a lost fish simply because you weren't willing to invest a little money and time replacing old, haggard line with fresh line. And always use quality line. So what if it costs a little more? It'll cast better, it'll feature superior knot strength and durability, it'll make your fishing more enjoyable and productive, and it will provide you with peace of mind because it will be up to the challenge of conquering big fish. That's a boatload of benefits for only a little extra expense.

Before every trip, before tying on a swivel, hook, lure or rig, cut off the last 10 to 12 feet of line on the reel. This part of the line takes a lot of abuse and abrasion from rocks, wrecks, shells and sand, and it also gets rubbed against the bottom of the boat. It's bound to be worn or damaged from the previous fishing trip, so the smart thing to do is pull it off the reel and cut it off before it creates any problems.

Weakfish are an ideal candidate for light-tackle action with light-action rods, small spinning reels and light lines.

Sunlight burns more than your skin, it also fries fishing line. Exposure to sunlight damages and dries out monofilament. Whenever possible, store reels, and spools of new fishing line, in a cool, dark and dry place, away from direct sunlight.

Monofilament of about eight to 12-pound test is commonly used by anglers casting plugs, light bucktails and speck rigs for weakfish and speckled trout. Surfcasters tossing lures along the beachfront spool up with 12 to 17-pound test. When fishing areas with dense and abundant structure or grass-beds, use heavier line (12-pound test and even heavier if needed). For warier fish in areas of relatively open, shallow and/or clear water, lighter line (six to 10-pound test) is recommended. Berkley Vanish fluorocarbon is virtually invisible and avoids detection, even when used for super-wary weaks and specks in gin-clear shallow water. For finesse fly fishing presentations in these demanding conditions, Cortland has developed the 444SL Ghostip and 444SL Clear fly lines, and also camo fly lines. Hi-Seas Quattro ultimate camo line, featuring sections of line that are alternately black, red, green and blue, can be used when fish are extremely spooky.

In most fishing situations, it's usually a good idea to use the lightest line possible. While some line strength is sacrificed with lighter line, it's generally more fisherman-friendly than heavier line. The thinner diameter of lighter lines results in less air resistance for longer casts, and less water resistance. Stren's Magnathin line works great for anglers casting small plastics and lightweight lures to weaks and specks because its fine-diameter provides great casting distance with less drag in the water for better lure performance. Lighter monofilament is also easier to tie and handle.

For the ultimate sport with small specks, use 2, 4 or 6-pound line.

Mono of 12 to 17-pound test also works well for anglers drifting bait on bottom rigs, and jiggers bouncing bucktails and metals on the bottom in relatively shallow water of 15 to 35 feet deep. Deeper jigging usually requires stronger line of 17 to 20-pound test, which is also commonly used by anglers livelining spot, croaker, mullet and snapper bluefish. Party boat anglers fishing bait rigs and bottom bouncing with jigs typically use conventional tackle spooled with 17 to 20-pound test monofilament. It provides better control over hooked fish and helps to avoid tangles with other fishermen. When a mate with a net isn't handy, it features the strength to lift hooked fish up and out of the water and over the rail.

Superbraided lines, including Berkley Fire Line, Bass Pro Shops Excel Nitro line, JWA's SpiderWire lines, and Western Filament T.U.F. lines, have rapidly grown in popularity in recent seasons. These incredibly strong lines feature a thinner diameter than monofilament of comparable strength, providing for longer and accurate casts and less water resistance. While monofilament stretches to about 15 percent, superbraids have practically no stretch at all. No stretch provides a very significant increase in sensitivity that makes it possible to detect even the lightest strikes and taps. The lack of stretch also provides for very quick and strong hooksets. Some monofilament manufacturers have developed mono that have come very close to matching the sensitivity of superbraided lines. Two examples include Berkley's Sensithin line, and Stren's Sensor line. On the other hand, the 15 percent stretch factor of typical monofilament serves as a good shock absorber that is lacking in superbraids. Mono's stretch is more forgiving of angler error, and enables a hooked fish to dive, jump and violently shake its head to some degree without the line snapping or the hook tearing free from the fish. Superbraids are not as susceptible to damage from sunlight as are mono lines, and they do not absorb as much water (which weakens line) as does monofilament.

The thin diameter, no stretch and increased sensitivity of superbraids make them an excellent choice where an immediate hookset is required, such as when jigging, casting lures and fishing bait on bottom rigs. I recommend monofilament in situations where it's necessary to pause and give line before setting the hook (dropback), such as when livelining. That's because a superbraid's no-stretch not only makes it easier for anglers to detect strikes, it also enables fish to immediately detect resistance from the tackle and angler that will cause the fish to rapidly drop the bait. Stren High-Impact line is popular among jiggers and live bait fishermen because of its abrasion resistance and good knot strength.

Most weakfish trolling involves pulling bucktails, plastic lures and spoons on or near the bottom. Superbraids and wire line are both more expensive than mono but they do a great job of cutting through the water, taking lures deep and keeping them there. However, fishing with wire line is a unique fishing experience onto itself. Wire line, especially in the hands of those new to wirelining, has a tendency to kink and even break where it has kinked. It can easily tangle on the reel and create a mess that requires an incredible amount of time and patience to straighten out. Plus, some claim that the considerable effort and energy required for successful wire line trolling make it more like work than fishing. Western Filament has a lead core line with a small diameter that is used by some trollers who prefer not to use wire line. But make no mistake about it, wire line trolling is often tremendously effective on trophy weaks and specks because it presents lures on the bottom in deep water where big fish often feed.

When casting, trolling or bottom fishing, most anglers rig up with a monofilament leader between the main line and their lure, bait or rig. Leaders can serve several important purposes. They often provide extra strength and abrasion resistance, they can be practically impossible for fish to see or detect in the water, and anglers can grab the leader when lifting hooked fish out of the water.

When casting artificials on relatively light eight to 12-pound test monofilament or superbraided line, a 2- to 3-foot mono leader of 17

Special monofilament leader material is sold in 4-foot lengths for making rigs and for casting leaders.

to 20-pound test is usually used. Bait fishermen, jiggers and party boat anglers spooled up with 12 to 17-pound test will use leaders of 20 to 30-pound test, while leaders of up to 50-pound test are used by liveliners expecting to catch trophy fish, and by anglers fishing jetties, lighthouse rocks and other heavy structure. Trollers pulling lures on either superbraided line or wire line often use mono leaders of 15 to 30-pound test that are anywhere from three feet to 20 feet long, or even longer.

An Albright knot can be used to tie a mono leader directly to the mono, superbraided line or wire line on the reel. An Albright knot works especially well with long leaders because it's a narrow-profile knot that can be reeled through the rod guides and onto the reel. That makes it possible to reel a hooked fish close to the boat or onto a jetty or beach without having to grab the leader and to pull it in hand-over-hand for a considerable distance.

Another approach to adding a leader to a mono line involves tying a spider hitch in the main line to double the end of the line from the reel. Then the leader, which is about twice the pound test rating of the main line, is attached to the end of the double line via a surgeon's knot. The doubled line, and then the heavier mono leader, provide light-tackle anglers and surfcasters with the extra toughness needed when hooked fish bring the line into contact with rocks, bridge pilings, the bottom of the boat, and sand and shells.

A quality swivel can also be used to connect the main line to a leader. A clinch knot is usually used to attach both the main fishing line and the heavier leader to the swivel. While some fishermen like this approach, others reject the need for additional hardware (the swivel) as unnecessary.

Weakfish and speckled trout are notoriously wary and can often be extremely leader shy. To overcome this, use camouflage line for leaders. Seaguar's fluorocarbon is a popular leader material, as it features almost the same refractive index as water, so it virtually disappears underwater, even when used in extremely clear water. If tuna fishermen use fluorocarbon leader to deceive sharp-sighted yellowfin and bluefin tuna, you know it'll work well on weaks and specks. Fluorocarbon is very dense and sinks faster than monofilament of the same diameter. It also offers superior knot strength, high abrasion resistance, and extreme sensitivity. Two drawbacks have been its expense, plus its stiffness can make it difficult to tie knots in fluorocarbon. However, easier-to-tie fluorocarbon leader material has been developed. In fact, Seaguar also markets CarbonPro, and Bass Pro Shops also makes available affordably-priced fluorocarbon line (not just leader material), both of which can be both spooled directly onto spinning and casting reels.

Hooks

"A recurved length of metal wire which terminates in a sharp point for the purpose of catching fish." That perfect definition of a hook is provided by McClane's New Standard Fishing Encyclopedia, which also tells us that, "The fish hook is one of man's oldest tools." The earliest hooks were developed thousands of years ago, and by 3400 B.C., during the Bronze Age, "fishhooks made of bronze with barbed points and turned-down, flatted shank terminals with a hole in the flat were being made and used in Crete and neighboring countries." A fish hook may seem like a rather simple device, yet improvements in design and manufacturing continue to this day. However, just like fishing line, hooks are very important but often overlooked and under appreciated by many anglers. Correctly choosing and using the right hook at the right time dramatically improves the likelihood of getting bites, hooking up and catching fish.

Not too long ago, it was a good idea to sharpen every hook before even using it. Now that's no longer necessary, and in fact may be counterproductive. High-tech hook sharpening procedures used by many manufacturers make hooks so sharp and strong that anglers can only diminish their sharpness by using a sharpening stone or file on them. Mustad uses its three-stage computer controlled Opti-Angler sharpening technology to ensure its Ultra Point hooks are super sharp fresh from the box. Many hooks are also chemically

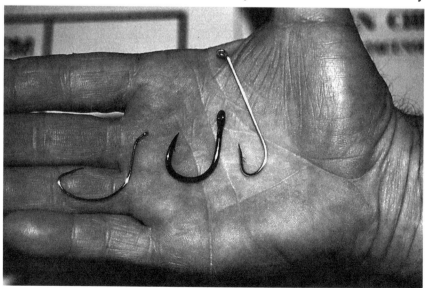

Fish hooks come in a variety of shapes and sizes, and each has a specific purpose. Here are several variations of weakfish bait hooks.

sharpened to a point that an angler simply can't match. However, an angler should use a stone or file to touch up a hook after it has been used for awhile, after several fish have been caught on it, and especially if it has been momentarily snagged and then freed and retrieved. Sharpen, or even replace a hook if there have been bites but few successful hookups.

When it comes to hook size, the primary consideration should be the size of the bait, not the size of the fish that are expected to be caught. A small bait needs to be fished on a small hook so it will have a realistic or natural appearance. Big weakfish and speckled trout will eat small baits and they can be subdued on small hooks, but fish usually won't strike small baits fished on big cumbersome hooks. Fishing a large bait on a small hook isn't effective because during the hookset, a big bait will probably interfere with or even prevent the hook from penetrating the fish's mouth, resulting in poorly-hooked or missed fish. Hook sizes 1/0 to 2/0 are generally recommended when fishing very small baits for weakfish and speckled trout, and/or when fishing for spooky fish in clear water. These small hooks will also catch sea bass, porgies (scup), croaker and other small fish that will eat baits intended for weaks and specks. Hooks in sizes 3/0 to 5/0 are probably the most commonly used in most weakfish and speckled trout fishing situations. Big hooks to 7/0 can be used when livelining spot, snapper bluefish and other live baits.

Wide-gap hooks, which get a lot of play among summer flounder fishermen, and also Chestertown, O'Shaughnessy, Siwash and Sproat hooks are used frequently to fish the baits most regularly used for weakfish and speckled trout. Wide-gap hooks are used a lot in pre-tied bait-fishing rigs found in tackle shops, such as Captain Frank Mitchell's famous Delaware Bay Green Machines, Pop's rigs, Wet Harley rigs, and other popular bottom rigs.

Baitholder-style hooks feature two barbs that stick out from the back of the shank of the hook. The barbs help hold soft baits - bloodworms, seaworms and clams - up on the hook and prevent them from sliding down and balling up at the bend of the hook. Bloodworms intended for weaks and specks are commonly threaded on Eagle Claw baitholder hooks, and other similar hooks, in size 2/0. When baiting up with three or four sand fleas, the fleas are threaded on and slid up the long shanks of Chestertown and Pacific Bass hooks. Short-shank bait hooks are the best choice for offering up live baits to weaks and specks. Straight-eye hooks can be tied to the leader or line with a Palomar knot or improved clinch knot, while hooks with down-turned eyes are usually snelled. Gamakatsu now markets colored hooks which can be matched to the color of the bait, and also fluorescent hooks that help attract fish and trigger strikes.

Circle Hooks

It can be argued that circle hooks may be the greatest single development ever made in fisheries conservation. The name "circle hook" comes from the hook's curved point. The point of a circle hook curves in and reduces the gap between the hook point and shank, and that design has been a lifesaver. Circle hooks are highly recommended when there's a strong possibility that undersized fish may be caught and will have to be released, or anytime an angler may decide to return fish, small or large. Believe it or not, circle hooks were first used by longliners because fish stayed hooked for the long periods between hauls. But it's saving fish, the opportunity to catch, unhook and release fish unharmed, not killing them, that has made circle hooks such a big hit among recreational anglers.

The beauty of circle hooks is that they go right to the fish's jaw. Fish are hooked in the corner of the mouth where they can be quickly and easily unhooked and released without injury. When fishing with circle hooks, do not set the hook very hard when there's a strike. A mild to moderate hookset is all that is necessary. Some anglers don't set the hook at all, they simply start reeling when

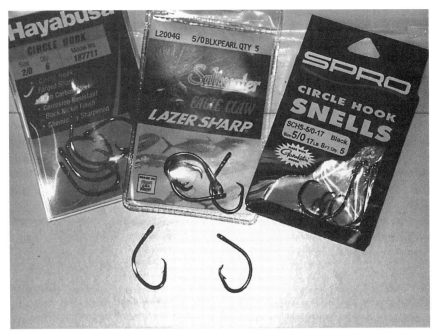

In recent years, circle hooks have become popular among conservation-minded fishermen, as they hook the fish in the corner of the mouth, enabling it to be released without injury.

there's a bite. This pulls the hook out of the fish's throat and pulls it around to where it hooks the fish in the jaw or corner of the mouth. Unlike traditional J-shaped hooks, circle hooks almost never hook a fish inside the mouth, in the throat or deep in the gills. And despite what may be considered the rather odd shape of circle hooks, most anglers experienced with them report no decrease in their number of strikes and hookups.

A number of companies manufacture and market circle hooks that can be used for weakfish and speckled trout fishing. Eagle Claw's L197G Sea Guard, VMC's 9788PS, and Mustad's 39960ST and 39965D are among the more popular light-wire circle hooks. The Owner Mutu Light Circle hook is a light-wire hook that's perfect when fishing small baits on lighter line for weaks and specks. Owner also makes available a slightly heavier wire circle hook that holds live baits while allowing them to swim naturally.

Sinkers

Use sinkers that are just heavy enough to get the bait or rig to the bottom and hold it there. Sinkers that are heavier than necessary are cumbersome to fish with and very possibly could reduce the catch. Sinkers aren't always used just to sink a bait or rig to the bottom, as sometimes they're intended to provide a natural presentation by getting them just beneath the surface or to very slowly sink a bait or lure as it's carried along with the current. The depth of the water and strength of the current are obviously important factors in determining how much weight is needed. So are the type of fishing line being used, and its diameter. Thinner lines meet with less water resistance, sink faster, and stay on or near the bottom longer than heavier lines. Ten-pound test line with a three-ounce sinker will get to the bottom much more quickly than 20-pound test with the same three-ounce sinker in the same conditions and depth. Superbraided lines are considerably thinner in diameter than monofilament of the same test, and therefore require lighter sinkers. Weakfish and speckled trout fishermen chumming and fishing with grass shrimp may require additional weight of only one-eighth-ounce or one-quarter-ounce, while trollers pulling lures and baits down deep may rig up with sinkers that weigh nearly two pounds.

Perhaps the most widely-used sinker of all, teardrop-shaped bank sinkers are attached to bait rigs to keep them on or near the bottom. Boating anglers slip or clip them on high/low rigs and other bottom rigs that are drifted over shoals, sloughs, channels and dropoffs. The smooth surface on bank sinkers helps them to avoid snagging on rocks, shells and other obstructions on the bottom, an especially important advantage when drift fishing as numerous potential snags may be encountered. Surf fishermen, and anglers on piers, docks and bridges also use bank sinkers to hold their bait rigs on the bottom.

However, a strong current, or breaking waves and water receding off the beach, may cause a bank sinker to roll around on the bottom. To better anchor their rigs to the bottom, surfcasters will often use pyramid sinkers. The name "pyramid" refers to their shape, and these three and four-sided sinkers that are flat on one end with a point on the other hold their ground in strong currents and in tumbling and swirling water. For even more bottom-grabbing power, use storm sinkers, which are pyramid sinkers that have a couple of pieces of short, stiff wire sticking out of them. The wire digs into the sand or mud for an even better grip on the bottom. Pyramid sinkers (not storm sinkers) are often used on fish-finder rigs because they feature a small wire eye on the flat end that fits well and can be easily slipped onto the sinker-holding clip on a fish-finder.

Egg sinkers are threaded onto the line from the reel. A barrel swivel is tied to the end of the line, and the leader is tied to the other end of the swivel. The swivel blocks the egg sinker from sliding down the leader to the hook. Weakfish and speckled trout anglers often use egg sinkers when fishing live baits. Egg sinkers and fish-finder

Different weights have different functions, and the desired presentation should determine which style is used.

rigs are similar in that as a fish grabs the bait and begins to move off with it, line is pulled through the egg sinker or fish-finder sleeve. The sinker is not dragged and the fish does not detect extra weight or resistance from the sinker. Small, lightweight egg sinkers and rubber core sinkers are often used to provide just enough weight to a chumming rig to get the bait down in a strong current. The chumming rig shouldn't sink straight to the bottom, but should fall slowly through the water as the current carries it with the chum.

Weakfish and speckled trout trollers use drail weights, also known as trolling sinkers, cigar sinkers and in-line sinkers, to get bucktails, plugs and spoons down deep where the big fish feed. Since in-line trolling sinkers are slender, some bottom bouncers use them on baited rigs, especially when fishing in rocks, wrecks and other structure where their slim profiles may avoid some of the snags that would be common with bulkier sinkers. Getting back to trolling, some anglers pull artificial lures and strip baits on three-way swivel rigs, and tie off to the bottom eye of the swivel a big dipsey sinker that holds the rig near the bottom. Depending on the depth of the water, strength of the current, and the type of line being used, drails and dipseys up to 24 ounces are used for weakfish and speckled trout trolling.

Some artificial lures can be effectively used as sinkers. Hooking a grass shrimp on a tiny shad dart is a great way of providing just enough weight to slowly sink the lightweight shrimp and provide a natural presentation in a strong current. In relatively shallow water, or at times of little wind and current, sinkers on bottom rigs can be replaced with bucktails or jigs of comparable weight. Not only will they pull the rig to the bottom, they'll also bring extra visual attraction and fish-appeal to the rig - I've never seen a weakie or speck try to eat a sinker, but they'll jump all over bucktails and jigs!

To improve catch success and make for a more enjoyable fight, sinkers should only be heavy enough to get a bait on the bottom and keep it there.

Snaps And Swivels

Snaps provide convenience. They connect a lure, rig or hook to the end of the line, and snaps make it possible to quickly and easily change these items by snapping them on and off without cutting line and tying knots. Some snaps, such as the popular Duolock snap, enhance the action of many artificial lures by allowing them to swim freely at the end of the line. A loop knot tied in the leader would also do this, but with a knot the line needs to be cut and another knot tied when the lure is changed.

Barrel swivels are commonly used to connect a leader to the main line from the reel; the line is tied to one eye of the swivel and the leader to the other eye. The other end of the leader may hold a bucktail, jig, plug or hook. A bottom rig, livelining rig or trolling rig can also be attached to the line via a barrel swivel. When casting bucktails and plugs, an Albright knot can be used instead of a swivel to tie a leader and the line directly together. The Albright is a narrow knot that can be reeled through the rod guides and onto the reel, making it possible to more easily cast and fish with a longer leader; an angler can also reel down right to a hooked fish. A barrel swivel can come only as far as the rod tip, leaving the leader hanging from the rod where it can create some problems when casting, and boating and landing hooked fish. Yet a good-quality ball-bearing swivel prevents line twist as a bait or lure is trolled, cast, jigged and retrieved.

Weakfish and speckled trout fishermen most frequently use three-way swivels to make bottom rigs and trolling rigs. The line from the reel is tied to one eye of the swivel. A leader with a hook or lure on the other end is tied to a second eye of the swivel. Tied to the bottom eye of the swivel is a leader that holds the sinker.

Some snaps and swivels, especially ball-bearing swivels, cost considerably more than others. That's because their components and construction make them significantly better than the less expensive ones. Buy the better snaps and swivels - don't subject yourself to the frustration of twisted line, or to the potential agony of a lost trophy fish, due to a failed snap or swivel, simply because you had decided to save a few cents. Fishing involves a considerable investment of time, effort and money, and it makes no sense whatsoever to cut corners when it comes to important terminal tackle like snaps and swivels.

Other important considerations include matching the size of the snap to the lure. A snap that's too large will interfere with the action and performance of some plugs and lures. Black snaps and swivels won't reflect light and will not spook weakfish and speckled trout.

Fly Fishing

With the proper tackle and presentations, fly fishermen can catch weaks and specks in all of their favorite haunts, from shallow back bay areas to deep water in our bigger bays and along the ocean-front. As with other types of fishing, the flyrodders who consistently catch the most fish are those who develop a comprehensive under-standing of their quarry and how the fish are affected by tide, cur-rent, structure, weather, and the availability of bait.

Weakfish and speckled trout are caught on Clouser minnows, Deceivers, Whistlers, Seducers, Bend Backs and shrimp patterns. Productive colors include chartreuse-over-white with lots of flash material, chartreuse-over-yellow with copper and red flash material, green-over-white, and blue-over-white. For shrimp patterns, try white, root beer or pink. An advantage of Clouser minnows, Bend Backs, and also shrimp patterns tied Clouser style, is that they ride through the water with the hook up, which reduces snagging in grass. Tie them on with a 100 Percent Loop Knot that enables the fly to swim freely at the end of the leader.

Seven, 8 and 9-weight rods provide anglers with the casting com-fort, distance and accuracy they need for most weakfish and speckled

Fly fishermen equipped with proper tackle can catch weakfish and speckled trout in all the same places normally frequented by anglers using conven-tional tackle.

trout fly fishing situations. These rods are capable of slugging it out with and subduing big, strong fish. Use 7 and 8-weight rods in shallow water, while 9-weight rods will get the job done in deeper water.

Bill May is an outdoor writer from Maryland who has fly fished around the world for dozens of fresh and saltwater species. For specks in grass-beds and other shallow-water locations, he recommends a floating line with a nine-foot tapered leader and a Bend Back tied on a 1/0 or 2/0 long-shank Mustad 34011 hook. Some anglers prefer an intermediate or running line which is attached with a loop-to-loop connection to a sinking tip. This set-up makes it possible to quickly change tips to adjust exactly how fast the fly will sink.

Popping plugs will also provoke strikes. May favors a popper-and-dropper rig in shallow water. It's somewhat similar to a teaser rig that surf fishermen or bottom jiggers would use. The popper-and-dropper rig features a typical fly fishing popper, with an 18-inch piece of mono leader tied to the popper's hook. A 1/50-ounce Clouser minnow is tied to the other end of the mono. Casting is easier with a 9-weight rod and this tandem rig, with a popper followed closely by a Clouser, will trigger seatrout strikes.

In deeper water, May casts a 1/36-ounce Clouser tied on a Mustad 34007 hook. It's fished on a slow-sinking or intermediate sinking line; the Scientific Anglers Stillwater line is a clear slow-sinking line that will not become stiff in cold weather. A level, three to five-foot leader of 12-pound test is used. An 8-weight rod with a 250 to 300 grain fast-sinking line should allow for effective presentations in deeper water. A retrieve that moves the fly slowly and erratically (start and stop, dive and dart) along the bottom will usually result in the most strikes.

Heavier sink tips are needed in a strong current and/or deep water. The line and fly should sink evenly, and when this occurs the fly can be retrieved along the bottom for the greatest possible distance. In very deep water, an angler can allow the fly to fall to the bottom and then jig it as if it were a bucktail or metal jig.

Tom Pagliaroli, an outdoor writer and light-tackle and fly fishing enthusiast from New Jersey, walks the sedge banks in his home state during a dropping tide and casts to weakfish with an 8-1/2-foot, 6 or 7-weight rod. He uses a sinking tip line with a nine-foot Seaguar fluorocarbon leader and small Clouser minnows or Furmisky's Shine Tails.

Sometimes practically no retrieve at all is needed to catch weaks and specks. Flyrodders casting to lighthouse rocks or jetties hook up while allowing the current to move and work the fly along the structure.

Chapter Three

PROVEN KNOTS AND RIGS

Fishing knots are the most vital connection between angler and fish - don't take them for granted. It's important to tie the correct knot when attaching a hook, lure, swivel or leader, and when tying up rigs and leaders. No matter what distractions exist when a knot is needed, including a red hot bite, a smart and successful angler will always take the time and put forth the concentration and effort needed to properly tie a knot and to inspect it for any possible imperfections. Choosing the proper knot for the task at hand, and carefully tying each and every knot, can easily be the difference between success and failure on the fishing grounds.

Always allow enough line when tying a knot so the loops and twists in a knot can be easily formed with a few inches of line left over. All twists, coils and spirals should be uniform so that when the knot is drawn snug, the turns will all tighten to the same degree. When tying knots with monofilament or superbraided lines, before the knot is drawn tight, briefly bring the knot to the lips and mouth where it can be quickly wetted with a small amount of saliva. This lubrication helps eliminate friction and enables the knot to be tightened smoothly and evenly. Don't jerk when tightening knots, always pull knots with steady, even pressure.

Use a fingernail clipper to cut line and the tag end of knots. A knife can accidentally nick the knot or line. Never use a lit cigarette to burn a small nub on the tag end in an attempt to prevent the tag end from slipping under the knot coils. The heat from the cigarette could weaken the coils and result in a knot that fails under pressure. Besides, if a knot is properly tied, it won't slip and will not need a nub on the tag end.

Frequently check all knots, plus the leader and line, for chafing, abrasion and nicks, and immediately re-tie damaged knots and replace worn line. Inspect the eyes on hooks, swivels, lures and anything that will be attached to the line or leader to be sure they are not damaged and will not nick or fray the knot, line or leader. Look over the rod guides to check for rough spots that could damage fishing line and result in lost fish.

The longest possible life span of a knot should be one fishing trip. Always cut off each knot, and the last few feet of leader or line, after each trip. Practice tying the knots to be presented in this chapter. These knots should cover most aspects of weakfish and speckled trout fishing. The knots in this chapter are used to attach a hook, lure, swivel or teaser to the line, to join two lines together, to tie loops in line, and to attach a leader to the end of the line.

Improved Clinch Knot

When many of us were youngsters, the improved clinch was the first fishing knot we were taught to tie. It's easy and strong (up to 98 percent of the breaking strength of the line) and it is one of the most widely-used knots in fishing. For many anglers it is the knot of choice when tying swivels, hooks and lures to the end of the line, especially monofilament up to 30-pound test. (It is not recommended that an improved clinch knot be tied in superbraided line. Instead, see Palomar knot.)

While an improved clinch is easy to tie, attention and care are required with each knot. An important factor with the improved clinch knot is the number of twists that are made around the standing line. Always make at least five twists, but no more than seven. Fewer than five twists will result in a weak knot, while too many twists may cause the knot to jam –and weaken– as it is pulled tight.

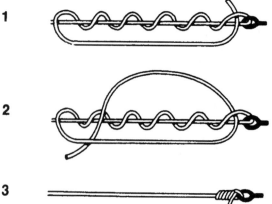

1

2

3

1. Pass the line through the eye of a swivel, hook or lure. With the end of the line, make five twists around the standing line. Pass the tag end through the loop formed at the eye of the hook.

2. A large loop is created when the tag

end is passed through the loop at the eye of the hook. Now pass the tag end through that large loop.
3. While holding the standing line and the free end, pull the coils tight. Make sure the coils lie next to each other and are not criss-crossed.

When tying an improved clinch knot in heavy mono leader of 50-pound test and heavier, it is often difficult to get the coils to draw up tightly. In this case, four twists (instead of five) can be used when tying the knot. The knot will be slightly weakened but it will still be stronger than the main line from the reel that the heavy leader is attached to.

In heavy leader, some anglers will tie a clinch knot instead of an improved clinch. The only difference is that with a clinch knot, the tag end is not passed through the large loop as described in step 2 (the knot is tightened after five twists are made and the tag end is passed through the loop that is formed at the eye of the hook).

Palomar Knot

In big-money largemouth bass tournaments, a single fish may mean tens of thousands of dollars in winnings and endorsements. Every bass is crucial, and the pros nail them with powerful, rock 'em sock 'em hooksets. The Palomar knot is an easy-to-tie knot with the strength to stand up to the abuse of explosive hooksets. It has caught on in a big way among saltwater fishermen who appreciate the ease of tying the Palomar (even easier than an improved clinch) and also its strength and lack of slippage under the stress and strain created by big, hard-charging fish.

The Palomar is used in much the same way as an improved clinch knot, to attach something to the end of the line. In the case of weak-fish and speckled trout anglers, that usually involves swivels, hooks, bucktails, jigs, small plugs, shad darts and speck rigs. It can be a bit difficult to use with larger lures, because the final loop in the knot must be pulled over the item being attached to the line. Big plugs, especially those with dangling treble hooks, often hang up and foul as the loop is pulled over them (use an improved clinch instead).

Manufacturers of superbraided lines (Fire Line, Spider Wire and others) recommend that a Palomar knot be used when tying on a lure, swivel or hook. These lines are thin and slick, and an improved clinch knot tied in a superbraided line will likely slip and fail when under pressure. A properly-tied Palomar will not slip, even in super-braided lines. Some bass anglers, after tying a Palomar knot in a braided line, will take an additional step to fight slippage by adding a drop or two of Super Glue directly to the knot. However, that practice hasn't caught on among saltwater anglers. As with all other knots, the key is to tie the knot carefully, and to cut off and re-tie whenever a knot doesn't set properly.

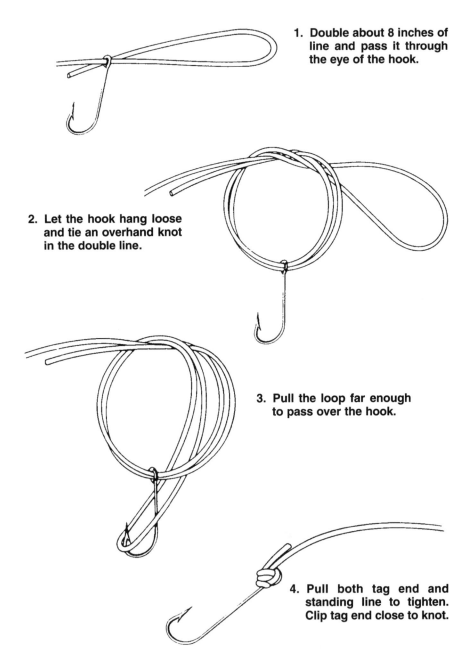

1. **Double about 8 inches of line and pass it through the eye of the hook.**

2. **Let the hook hang loose and tie an overhand knot in the double line.**

3. **Pull the loop far enough to pass over the hook.**

4. **Pull both tag end and standing line to tighten. Clip tag end close to knot.**

Uni-Knot

While more difficult to tie than an improved clinch or palomar knot, a uni-knot does provide a little more room for error in that a poorly-tied uni-knot will usually test out better than a poorly-tied clinch or Palomar. But because knots are such a critical connection between angler and fish, it's always important to strive for perfection when tying any type of knot. There simply is no excuse for a poorly-tied knot, and anyone who knowingly fishes a knot they could have tied better is risking heartbreak when that big fish shows up.

The time and effort required to learn how to properly tie a uni-knot are rewarded by the knot's superior strength which is 97 to 99 percent of the breaking strength of the line. The uni-knot was invented by Vic Dunaway, an outstanding and innovative angler, and editor of *Florida Sportsman* magazine. This versatile knot is used by everyone from light-tackle inshore fishermen to tuna and marlin anglers on the offshore grounds. Just like a Palomar and improved clinch, its application to weakfish and speckled trout fishing is that it is used to attach swivels, hooks, bucktails, jigs, small plugs, shad darts and speck rigs to the end of the line.

It is possible to leave a small loop between the knot and the lure or hook it's being tied to by not drawing the knot all the way against the eye of the lure or hook. Some bucktailers and jiggers prefer the small loop because they feel it provides their lure with more action by enabling it to swing more freely. The loop will disappear when the pressure of a hooked fish collapses the knot against the lure or hook.

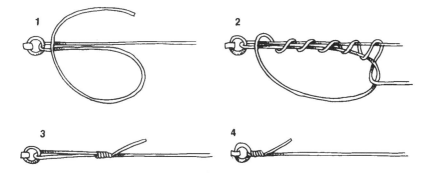

1. Run the tag end of the line through the eye of the hook at least 12 inches and fold it back against the standing line. Bring the tag end back as shown to form a loop.
2. Make six turns with the tag end around the two side-by-side lines and through the loop. Pull on the tag end and the standing line

to snug up the coils.

3. Pull on the hook and the main line to draw the knot close to the hook eye. Be sure to moisten the knot with saliva so the tightened coils will not fray or heat the main line as the coils are drawn down.

4. Continue pulling until the knot is good and tight.

Snelling A Hook

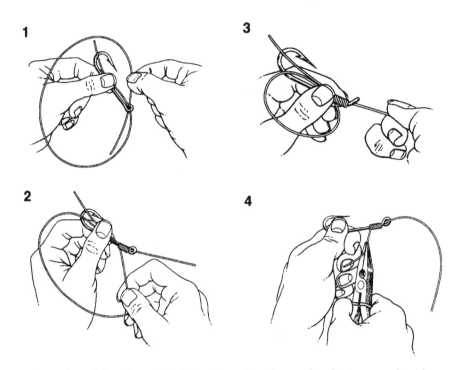

A vast variety of weakfish bottom rigs, from simple to complex, is available at tackle shops. They feature one hook or two, some come adorned with flashy spinnerblades, and fish-appeal is also provided by beads and bucktails in white, green, chartreuse, yellow, pink and purple. Just add bait, slip on a sinker, and these rigs are ready to catch fish. Yet many anglers enjoy purchasing their hooks, leaders and accessories separately, and using their own creativity, to tie up their own rigs. They also appreciate the reward and satisfaction that come with catching fish on rigs of their own creation. An important step in the process of tying up bottom rigs, and also live bait rigs, is snelling the hook to the leader.

1. Pass one end of the leader through the eye and past the hook

bend. Pass the other end of the leader through the eye in the opposite direction.
2. Hold both lines along the shank. Use the line hanging from the eye and wind tight coils around the shank and both lines, starting at the eye and working toward the bend. Make five or 10 neat turns.
3. Hold the coils and pull on the long leader end until the entire loop disappears under the coils, and pull the coils snug.
4. Hold the tag end with pliers and the leader in the other hand, and pull in opposite directions to tighten the snell securely. Clip off the tag end.

Dropper Loop

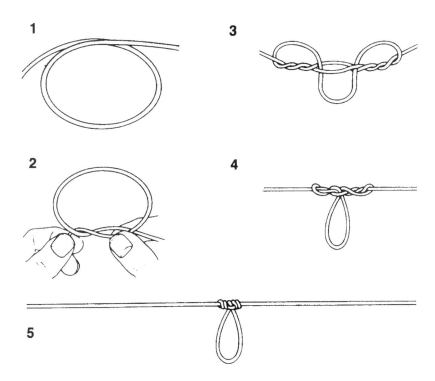

This knot, which is used to create a loop in a leader or line, has been on the fishing scene for a long time. It is still used today, commonly in bottom rigs for weakfish and other species, to conveniently form a loop that can be used to hold a hook, lure or teaser. On bottom rigs, a dropper loop is often used instead of a three-way swivel. A hook, lure or teaser can be put on the loop by slipping the loop through the eye and then over the hook, lure or teaser. Or, one leg of the loop can be cut near the main leader to create a single, longer leader onto which a hook, lure or teaser is tied. A fair degree of finger dexterity is required for this knot, but with a little practice it soon becomes easy to tie a dropper loop.

1. Form a loop in the line.
2. Pull one side of the loop down and begin taking turns with it around the standing line. Keep the point where the turns are made open so there are an equal number of turns on each side.
3. After eight or 10 turns, reach through the center opening and pull the main loop through, as shown. Put your finger through this loop so it won't slip back.
4. Hold the loop with your teeth and pull both strands of line, creating tight coils.
5. Release the loop and pull hard to set the knot. The tightening coils will cause the dropper to stand out perpendicular to the line.

Surgeon's End Loop

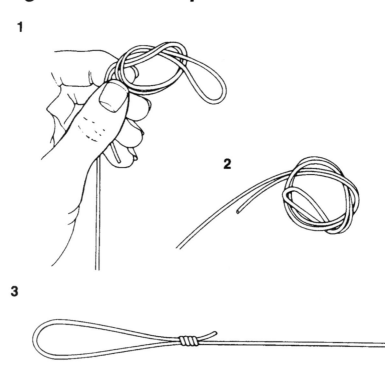

While the dropper loop just described creates a loop in the middle of a line, a surgeon's end loop is tied to form a loop at the end of a line. This loop is frequently used on bottom fishing rigs to hold the sinker. Slipping a sinker on this loop is much better than tying it directly to the rig because as the wind, water depth and tidal conditions change, and more or less weight is needed, it is quick and easy to slip one sinker off and another sinker onto the loop, instead of cutting and retying another sinker to the rig.

1. Double back a few inches of line and tie it in an overhand knot.
2. Leave the overhand knot open and bring the doubled line through once again.
3. Hold the standing line and tag end and pull the loop to tighten the knot. The size of the loop formed can be controlled by positioning the loose knot and holding it while the knot is tightened. Clip tag end.

Albright Knot

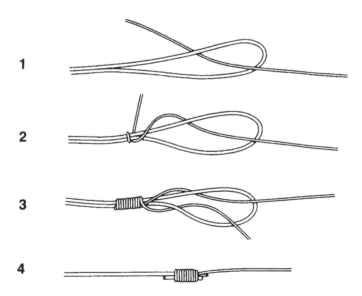

This knot is used to add a heavier leader to a lighter line. Weakfish bucktailers, plugcasters and jiggers can use it to attach a 30-pound or 50-pound test mono leader to the 12, 17 or 20-pound test mono on the reel. An Albright knot can also be used to tie a mono leader to the end of a superbraided line. When connecting leader to line, an Albright knot provides a very significant advantage over a swivel. The Albright is a narrow-profile knot that will easily pass through the guides on most rods, and it will enable anglers to tie on long leaders and to reel down more closely to a hooked fish.

Some surfcasters use an Albright to tie a heavier mono shock leader to the mono on their reels. This heavier leader will stand up better to abrasion as the line comes into contact with sand, rocks, shells and hooked, struggling fish. Some practice time is required before this knot is mastered, but it's worth it.

1. Double back a few inches of the heavy line and pass about 10 inches of the lighter line through the loop.
2. Wrap the light line back over itself and both strands of the heavy line. This is a bit easier if you hold the light line and both leader strands with your left thumb and forefinger, and wind with your right hand.
3. Make 10 snug, neat wraps, then pass the end of the line back through the original big loop, as shown.
4. While holding the coils in place, pull gently on both strands of the heavy line, causing the coils to move toward the end of the loop. Take out the slack by pulling on both strands of light line. When the knot is snug, pull hard on the main line and main heavy line. Pull as hard as possible for a good, solid knot. Clip both excess tag ends close.

Spider Hitch

Used everywhere from tuna canyons to rainbow trout pools, a spider hitch creates a double line at the end of the line, and it's an excellent knot for weakfish and speckled trout anglers to know. A doubled line doubles the strength of the line and helps fight abrasion and break-offs, and many anglers double the end of their main fishing line before tying a leader on it. The knot commonly used to connect a doubled main line and leader is a surgeon's knot (which we'll discuss next). While easy to tie, a surgeon's knot will weaken the main line by as much as 25 percent, so it is a good idea to first provide additional strength in the main line by doubling it up with a spider hitch.

While a strong Albright knot can be used to connect a leader to a lighter line without doubling up on the lighter line, many anglers find the Albright difficult and time-consuming to tie, so they instead use the spider hitch and surgeon's knot to attach a leader. Like the Albright knot, the spider hitch comes into play for weakfish and speckled trout anglers when increasing line strength and adding a leader for bucktailing, jigging, casting plugs and bottom fishing.

The length of the double line and leader can vary from anywhere from a few inches to feet to yards, depending on the fishing. First attempts at tying a spider hitch may make you feel like you're all thumbs, but stick with it and it won't be long until you have it mastered.

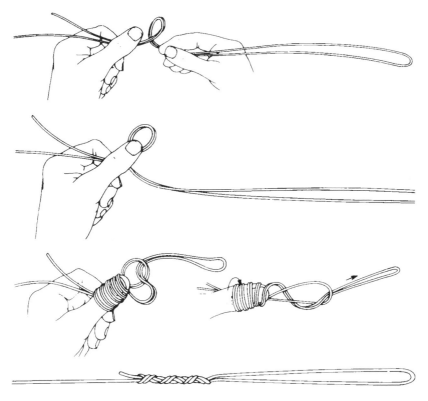

1. Create the desired length of doubled line by folding the line back. Near the tag end, twist the strands into a small reverse loop.
2. Hold the small loop between your left thumb and forefinger, with the thumb extended well above the finger.
3. Wind the double line strands around your thumb and loop strands, taking five parallel turns. Pass the end of the original big loop through the small loop, pull the slack out, and pull the five turns off your thumb. Moisten with saliva, and slowly pull the tag end and standing line strands against the loop strands to tighten the knot. The coils should be even (if they wrap back over themselves then it's necessary to try the knot again). For final tightening, pull the standing line only against the loop.

Surgeon's Knot

This knot can be used to join two lines of different diameters (see spider hitch knot). It is easy to learn, easy to tie and convenient for adding heavy leaders for jigging, livelining, surfcasting and plugcasting.

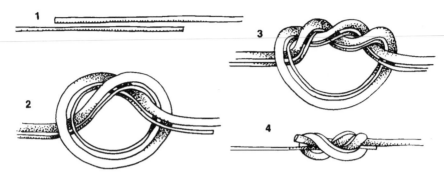

1. Lay the line and leader parallel with an overlap of about 8 inches.
2. Treat the two lines as a single line and tie an overhand knot, passing the entire leader through the loop. Leave the loop open.
3. Make a second overhand knot, again passing the whole leader and overlapped line through.
4. Hold both overlaps and pull in opposite directions to make the knot. Then pull the line only against the leader to set the knot. Clip the surplus ends close to the knot.

Haywire Twist

The haywire twist is an important knot for anglers who troll deep for big weakfish with wire line, as it provides a strong connection

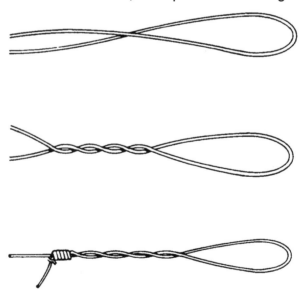

when attaching a swivel, bucktail or mono leader to wire line.

1. Pass several inches of the tag end of the wire through the eye of a swivel or bucktail. Bend the tag end back and cross it over the standing wire to form a small loop.
2. Hold the loop firmly with the thumb and forefinger of your left hand. Both sections of wire must be twisted simultaneously, or else the tag will simply wrap around the standing wire and produce a much weaker connection.
3. Make at least 3-1/2 twists in the two wires. Next, bend the tag end so it is 90 degrees to the standing wire.
4. Hold the already-twisted section and wrap the tag end around the standing wire in several neat, tight, parallel coils.
5. Bend the last inch or so of the tag to the right angle, bending away from the standing line, not over it, to form a "handle".
6. Hold the twist steady and rock the tag end back and forth. It should break quickly, leaving a smooth end at the twist. If the wire is cut at this stage of the twist, it will leave a sharp burr that can cut your hand.

High/Low Rig

The double-hook high/low rig is very popular for fishing chunks of shedder crab, squid strips, cut spot and other baits on and near the bottom.

A three-way swivel is tied to the end of the line. A 2 to 4-foot leader of 20 or 30-pound test is tied to the bottom eye of the swivel, and another small three-way swivel is tied to the end of this leader. On the remaining eye of the top swivel, tie on a 12-inch to 18-inch leader that has a 3/0 to 5/0 wide gap hook, or Chestertown or O'Shaughnessy hook, tied or snelled on the end of it. On the bottom swivel, attach a short length of monofilament to the bottom eye; tie a surgeon's end loop at the end of that mono to hold the sinker. Finally, a leader of about 24 to 30 inches with a hook on the end is tied to the other eye of the bottom swivel.

It's important that the distance between the top leader and bottom leader is greater than the length of the top leader. This prevents the hook and bait on the top leader from sagging down and fouling with the bottom leader.

Some anglers will use light monofilament of about eight to 12-pound test at the very bottom of the rig to hold the sinker. When a rig gets snagged on the bottom or in structure, it's often the sinker that gets hung up. If the sinker can't be worked free of the snag, then the angler applies pressure to the rig and the breaking point should

HIGH-LOW BAIT RIG

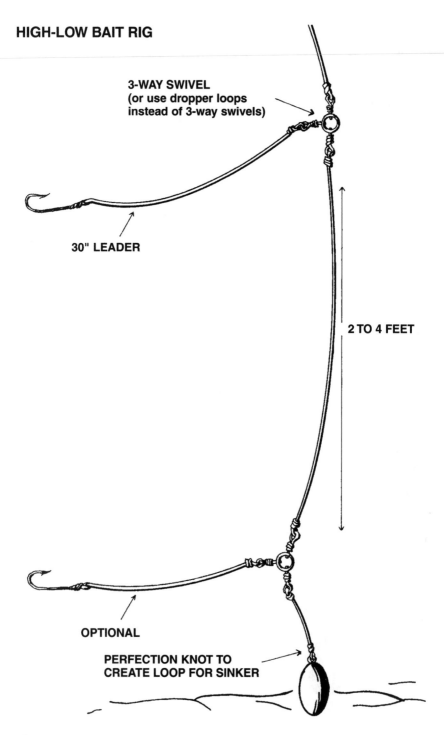

**3-WAY SWIVEL
(or use dropper loops
instead of 3-way swivels)**

30" LEADER

2 TO 4 FEET

OPTIONAL

**PERFECTION KNOT TO
CREATE LOOP FOR SINKER**

CAROLINA HIGH-LOW RIG

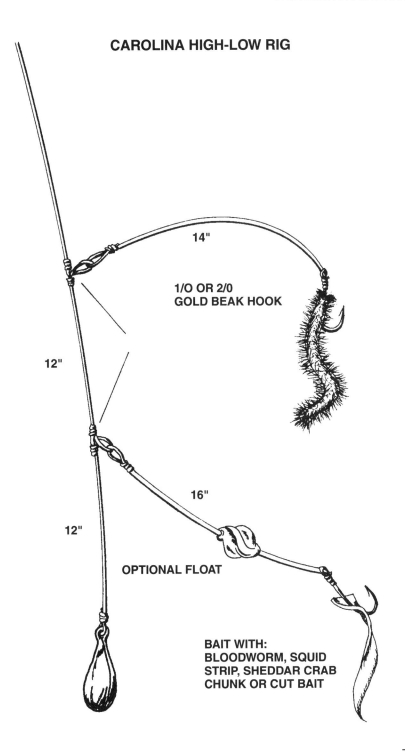

14"

1/O OR 2/0
GOLD BEAK HOOK

12"

16"

12"

OPTIONAL FLOAT

BAIT WITH:
BLOODWORM, SQUID
STRIP, SHEDDAR CRAB
CHUNK OR CUT BAIT

be the light mono. While the sinker is lost, the two hooks, baits and swivels will be saved. If snags are particularly frequent, one way to reduce them is to use a narrow-profile sinker, such a small in-line sinker or trolling drail, instead of a wider-profile bank sinker. Another snag-reduction effort that can be made is to remove one of the hooks and fish only one hook and bait at a time. Snags can be frustrating, yet these are often the types of areas that hold the most fish.

Instead of using three-way swivels, some anglers will tie two dropper loops in the main leader. Long loops can be tied and leaderless hooks are slipped directly onto the loops, or tie smaller dropper loops and use leadered hooks.

An obvious advantage of a high/low rig is the ability to fish a bait on or very near the bottom, and another bait just above the bottom. This increases the chances that at least one bait will be presented directly in front of feeding weakfish or speckled trout. A high/low rig also enables an angler to fish two different baits at the same time, which can be especially helpful when fish are finicky, or when determining the fish's preference at that particular time and location. Fluke are attracted to the same structure - shoals, sloughs, rocks, pilings - as weaks and specks. Many anglers will bait the bottom hook of a high/low rig with a long fluttering squid strip or cut bait intended specifically for fluke, while a chunk of shedder crab to tempt weaks or specks is put on the top hook.

Fish-Finder Rig

With a fish-finder rig, a fish can pick up the bait and begin to move off with it without dragging the sinker and without detecting the weight of the sinker. The no-resistance feature and simplicity of this rig make it very popular among fishermen, and weakfish and speckled trout anglers use it in one form or another to fish live baits, peeler crab chunks, squid strips and other baits from anchored boats, beaches, piers, jetties and bridges.

Fully-tied fish-finder rigs for a variety of species are available in many tackle shops. The fish-finders themselves can be purchased separately and they are nothing more than a short length of plastic sleeve with a clip attached that holds the sinker. The main line from the reel is threaded through the plastic sleeve, and then a swivel is tied to the end of the main line. A 2 to 4-foot leader with a hook tied or snelled on the end is then tied to the other end of the swivel. The swivel prevents the fish-finder with the sinker from sliding down the line to the hook, and it also prevents line twist if the bait was to spin in the water. When a fish grabs the bait, it will pull line through the

SURF FISH-FINDER RIG

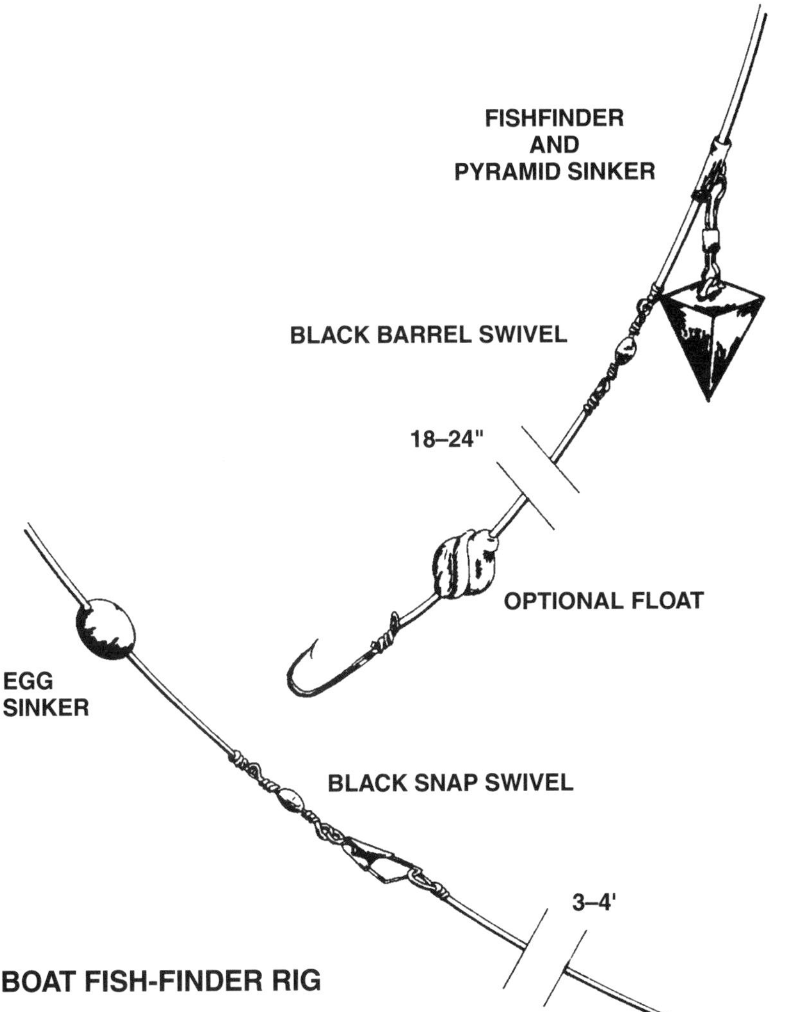

**FISHFINDER
AND
PYRAMID SINKER**

BLACK BARREL SWIVEL

18–24"

OPTIONAL FLOAT

**EGG
SINKER**

BLACK SNAP SWIVEL

3–4'

BOAT FISH-FINDER RIG

plastic sleeve on the fish-finder. The sinker is not dragged or moved in any way as line is pulled through the fish-finder. There's no sudden additional weight that can very easily spook a fish into dropping the bait. For this to occur with maximum efficiency, the angler must be alert and ready to play out line the instant there's a strike.

I have seen anglers take a shortcut when it comes to fish-finder rigs. They do not use the plastic sleeve and its attached clip; instead, they put the sinker directly on the line by threading the line through the hole in a bank sinker or through the eye of a pyramid sinker. I do not recommend this because even the tiniest rough edge on the sinker hole or eye can damage the line to the point where the line will be easily broken under the pressure of a hooked fish. On the other hand, there is little doubt that the inside of the plastic sleeve on a fish-finder is smooth and poses no threat to the line. Plus, fish-finders are so readily available and inexpensive that there really is no reason not to always have a handful in your tackle box. About the only feasible replacement for a fish-finder is a snap swivel; the line is run through the swivel eye and the sinker is clipped on at the snap. In shallow water, or when there is little or no current, or at other times when only a very light weight is needed, a sliding egg sinker can be slid on the line in lieu of a fish-finder. It's a good idea to first peer through the hole in the sinker to be sure it's smooth and free of any burrs or debris that could rub on the line and weaken it.

Some anglers, especially surf and pier fishermen soaking cut baits, prefer a fish-finder rig with a cork float on the leader just ahead of the hook. The float helps hold the bait slightly up and off the bottom, where it is away from bait-stealing crabs and where it can be more easily spotted by fish.

Fish-finder rigs are especially useful to weakfish and speckled trout anglers when fishing live baits such as spot, snapper blues, mullet and bunker. The rigs give the bait some mobility. Plus, with live baits, anglers should not set the hook the instant there's a strike. Instead, it's important to pause and play out line as the fish begins to swallow the bait. A fish-finder rig with the line sliding freely through a plastic sleeve enables weakies and specks to gobble down bait, and the angler to play out line, without interference from the rig. Then the angler reels in all slack - to the point where the weight of the fish is easily detected - and sets the hook with authority!

Three-Way Swivel Rig

A three-way swivel can be used to fashion a simple rig that effectively presents a bait near the bottom where weaks and specks will

RUBBER-CORE
WORM DRIFT RIG

THREE-WAY
SWIVEL RIG

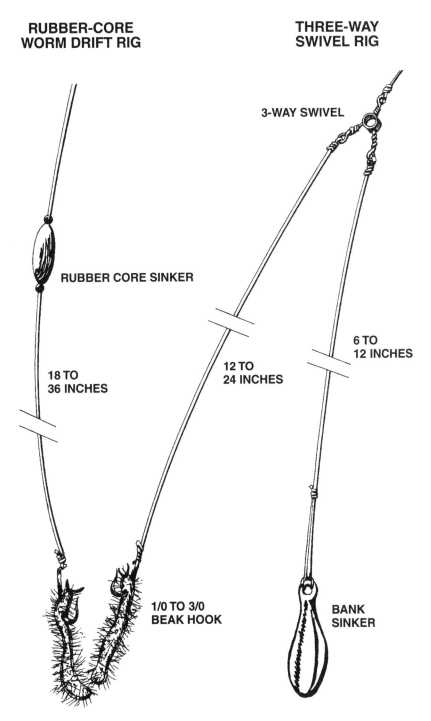

3-WAY SWIVEL

RUBBER CORE SINKER

6 TO
12 INCHES

18 TO
36 INCHES

12 TO
24 INCHES

1/0 TO 3/0
BEAK HOOK

BANK
SINKER

grab it. Tie the three-way swivel to the end of the line from the reel. To the bottom eye of the swivel, tie on a six to 12-inch length of mono. At the other end of the mono, tie a surgeon's end knot to form a loop; the loop holds the sinker. On the other swivel eye, tie on a 12 to 24-inch length of 20 to 30-pound test monofilament leader that has a 3/0 to 5/0 wide gap hook, or Siwash or Sproat hook, tied or snelled on the other end.

Live Bait Rig

A simple, straightforward rig is in order when targeting big weakfish and speckled trout with live spot, croaker, mullet, snapper bluefish or bunker. It involves tying a barrel swivel to the end of the line. Tie to the other end of the swivel a 16 to 24-inch length of 30-pound test leader (50-pound test may even be needed to better prevent line abrasion when fishing around hard, rocky structure). An Eagle Claw L197G Sea Guard circle hook, Mustad 39965D circle hook, VMC 9788PS circle hook, or other big 5/0 to 7/0 live bait hook, is tied or snelled to the end of the leader.

LIVE SPOT RIG

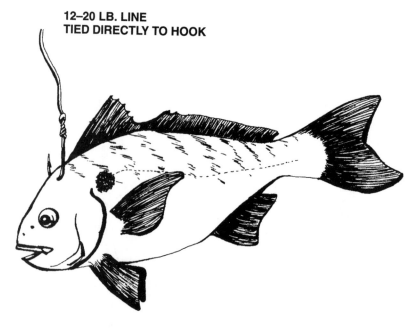

12–20 LB. LINE
TIED DIRECTLY TO HOOK

Live baits, when hooked and cast, almost always swim down to the bottom or toward nearby structure. Therefore, a sinker is usually not needed with a live bait rig, especially when fishing around jetties, lighthouses, bridge pilings and other structure. In deep water, or when drifting live baits in inlets or at other locations with a hard-running current, it may be a good idea to add a little weight to the rig in the form of a small drail, or small rubber-core sinker that is attached directly to the leader.

Live bait can be hooked in several ways. A common approach is to run the hook through the back of the baitfish just ahead of the dorsal fin. Some anglers prefer to hook the bait through the nostrils, or in the mouth and out through the top jaw.

Many anglers use a 5/0 to 7/0 live bait hook for this type of fishing, yet there are some who prefer a treble hook, and they hook the bait on one or two of the trebles. One advantage of a treble hook is that it makes it somewhat easier to hook a fish that has grabbed the bait, but on the other hand a treble hook more easily snags seaweed and other debris than does a single hook. With live bait, it's crucial to pause after a pickup and before setting the hook. When a fish grabs the bait and begins to move with it, the angler should give line and remain calm. Some say it's a good idea to count to five, but it's amazing how quickly people can count to five in the excitement of realizing a big fish has grabbed their bait. Nonetheless, not allowing enough time for the fish to get the bait well in its mouth before setting the hook will very often result in missed fish. During the drop-back, it's also important to play out line so the fish detects no resistance. It's a lot less cumbersome to let out line in this type of situation with a conventional reel than it is with a spinning reel. After a drop-back of at least 10 seconds, the angler should then carefully reel in all slack until the weight of the fish is felt on the line. The rod tip should then be pointed down at the water in the direction of the fish. Then set the hook hard and get to work reeling in a big weakfish or speckled trout.

Casting And Jigging Leader

This leader system involves three knots, a stretch of doubled line from the reel, and leader material, but it's simpler than it may sound. A spider hitch (or the more difficult Bimini twist) is tied in the main line to create a loop of doubled line at the end of the monofilament line from the reel. The leader is also monofilament about twice the pound test rating of the main line. The leader is attached to the doubled line from the reel with either an Albright knot or a surgeon's

CASTING AND JIGGING LEADER

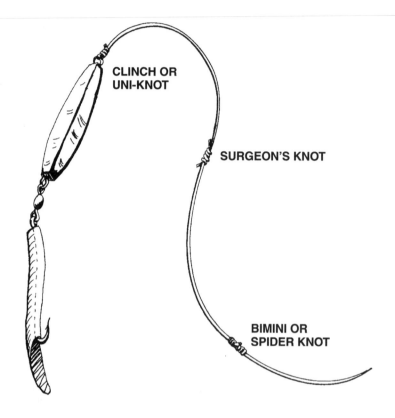

CLINCH OR
UNI-KNOT

SURGEON'S KNOT

BIMINI OR
SPIDER KNOT

knot. The Albright knot is the stronger of the two knots, but it's more difficult to tie. The surgeon's knot is easier to tie but weaker, yet because the knot is tied in the doubled main line, the surgeon's knot is stronger than the single line above the spider hitch. A Palomar or improved clinch knot is used to tie the lure to the end of the leader.

The casting and jigging leader works well in a variety of situations. Surfcasters tossing bucktails and plugs to weaks and specks use it as the heavier leader and doubled main line act as a shock absorber during casting, and stand up well to abrasion as a hooked fish may drag the line and leader across sandy bottom loaded with sharp shells. Light-tackle anglers will use this leader system when casting lures in inlets and around jetties and rockpiles that would damage lighter, single lines and leader. Deep-water jiggers also appreciate the toughness and durability this leader system provides, as the heavy leader and doubled line aren't easily damaged when a hooked fish scrapes it on the bottom of the boat or the landing net.

Bobber Float Rig And Popping Rig

Bobbers and floats aren't just for kids. As youngsters they served us well when catching bluegills and bass, and as adults there are times when bobbers and floats are just the ticket for big weaks and specks. A bobber float rig is pretty much the same set-up we used in freshwater years ago. A plastic or cork bobber is clipped on the line about two to four feet above a 3/0 to 5/0 hook. The bobber suspends the hook and bait just off the bottom, or just above a grass-bed. A small split shot may be added to the line about six to eight inches above the hook to help get the bait down in the water. Grass shrimp, small pieces of shrimp, squid strips or cut baits including spot, bluefish and mullet are commonly used on this simple yet effective rig. A bobber float rig can be used to present a bait in a chum slick, or the angler can allow the current to push the bobber and rig away from the boat and toward productive structure such as a jetty, dock, bulkhead or bridge piling.

A popping rig, especially popular among southern speckled trout anglers, is fairly similar to the bobber float rig, but the float differs from a bobber in that it features a forward end that's wide and

BOBBER RIG

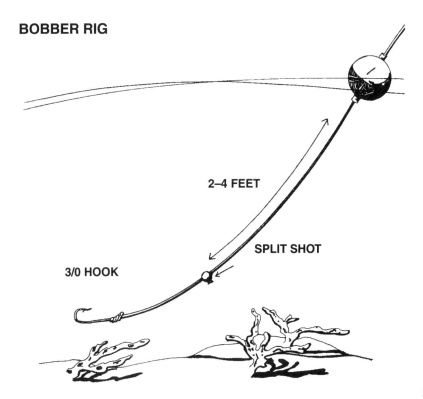

2–4 FEET

SPLIT SHOT

3/0 HOOK

concave, and the float tapers down to a more narrow rear end. The brightly-colored floats are usually available in orange or red. A shrimp is typically threaded onto the hook. The rig is cast and then retrieved by flicking the wrist and twitching the rod tip so that the concave end of the float enticingly pops, slurps and splashes as it comes across the surface of the water in a start-and-stop manner. This commotion, very much like a wounded baitfish struggling on the top of the water, attracts the attention of predatory speckled trout. When they come to investigate the noise they encounter the shrimp on the hook and inhale it.

Extra Enhancements

Many anglers like to add just a little bit extra to their rigs with the expectation that it will better catch the attention of fish and trigger more strikes. Some of these items serve important functions that go beyond fish appeal. While beads make a rig more colorful, they can also be used to protect knots. Thread one or more beads on the line or on a leader between a fish-finder rig and the swivel, or between an egg sinker and the swivel, and the beads will prevent the fish-finder or egg sinker from sliding into the knot and possibly weakening it.

Rig enhancements, like the addition of plastic beads, not only add visual appeal, but also protect the line and knots and can result in big catches of weakfish.

The spinnerblades and buzzblades that are common on many largemouth bass lures can also be used effectively in saltwater. When added to a bait rig and drifted along the bottom, the blades will spin and create flash and vibrations that can attract weakfish and speckled trout from considerable distances.

One of the most popular and productive innovations in recent years has been Worden's Spin-N-Glo. The leader is threaded through the Spin-N-Glo's small colorful plastic body which has two small blades attached. As the rig moves through the water, the blades spin the Spin-N-Glo and create eye-catching flash. It's a good idea to place one or more beads on the line between the Spin-N-Glo and the hook or lure. The beads will keep the Spin-N-Glo spinning freely by preventing it from catching on the knot. Spin-N-Glo rigs used in freshwater are very effective on salmon, walleye and bass, on saltwater bottom rigs they are deadly on fluke and stripers, and they also prompt strikes from weakfish and speckled trout.

Plastic skirts are also used to bring additional fish appeal to bait rigs. They are usually slipped on and over the hook so that at least part of the plastic skirt flutters behind the hook with the squid strip or other bait that may be used. Boone's squid skirts are especially popular among weakfish anglers.

Items that can be added directly to the hooks of bottom rigs, and fished either alone or in addition to the bait, include pork rind strips, felt strips, and scent and flavor-packed soft plastics such as Berkley Sandworms and Berkley Power Baits.

Rick Neumann, a surf fishing expert and writer for The Fisherman magazine's Mid-Atlantic Edition, ties his own unique bait rigs that have significantly increased his catch of weaks, specks and other species. Rick does not tie or snell hooks on his surf fishing bait rigs. Instead, he uses small Clark spoons, Tony Accetta spoons, or other small, lightweight spoons. A strip of squid, small chunk of peeler crab, bloodworm or other bait is then put on the hook of the spoon. The movement and flash of the spoon dangling from the bottom rig, plus the scent and flavor of the bait, create a combination that weaks and specks often cannot resist.

Chapter Four

FISHING WITH BAIT

Big, mature weakfish and speckled trout are high-order inshore predators. Their diet includes an amazingly wide variety of baitfish, worms, crustaceans and other critters. The marine environment is brutally harsh and unforgiving, and food isn't always easy to come by. Much of the time, practically anything weakfish and speckled trout can get in their mouth and down their throat is fair game.

These diverse food sources, and the weakfish and speckled trout that eat them, are found throughout the near-shore fishing grounds. The search for grass shrimp, sand fleas and minnows will often bring weakfish and speckled trout right to the feet of anglers on marsh banks in back bays, ocean beaches, docks, piers and bridges. In our bays and coastal waters, weakfish and speckled trout use shoals, sloughs and edges as feeding stations where they pick off crabs, shrimp and baitfish. Boating anglers use LORAN, GPS and DGPS, plus fishfinders, charts and log books, to locate and fish these bottom contours. Jetties, lighthouse rocks and wrecks provide hiding places and food for crabs, eels and fish, which then attract hungry weaks and specks, which in turn bring anglers to these productive fishing locations. The diversity of food sources in the weakfish and speckled trout diet, plus the many different types of locations where the food and fish are found, provide enjoyable and challenging fishing opportunities for anglers of all interests, skills and means. Everything from ultralight and fly fishing tackle to heavy-duty wire line trolling gear is used to successfully pursue and catch weakfish and speckled trout.

While weakfish and speckled trout are predators with extensive diets, they usually do not haphazardly devour just anything. For the sake of comparison, weakfish and speckled trout are much more like striped bass than they are bluefish, Spanish mackerel and false albacore. Blues, Spanish and little tunny are voracious predators that often use speed to chase down their prey. Weaks and specks are like striped bass in that they are usually less aggressive and more wary predators that prefer to stick close to structure such as shoals, edges, jetties, bridge pilings, rocks and wrecks, where they can sneak up on their meals, or ambush food as it washes by them in the current.

To trigger the most strikes, the size of the bait must closely match the size of the food that's most available to weaks and specks at that time. I'm convinced that many anglers who aren't as successful as they had hoped make the common mistake of fishing lures and baits that are considerably larger than the prevalent bait. As closely as possible, match the size of your bait or lure to the size of the available food source. When in doubt, go small. My experience has repeatedly indicated that baits and lures on the small side will consistently provoke more strikes than larger offerings.

Like other predators, weakfish and speckled trout at times can become very selective. If one type of bait is extremely prevalent, that may be all they'll want. For example, during the late summer and fall, weakfish often get turned on to live spot. It may be next to impossible to toss a live spot into the water without having it immediately devoured, while other normally productive live and cut baits, bucktails and swimming plugs, may be totally ignored.

Perhaps the weirdest case of this extreme selectiveness I have ever witnessed came during a vacation I took in North Wildwood in New Jersey one September in the late 1980s. Word was out that each afternoon big weakfish would make their way into Hereford Inlet on the incoming tide. Fishermen showed up in full force to get in on that action, and big numbers of impressive fish were caught for several consecutive days. Yet without fail, the vast majority of weaks was taken by anglers on the beach and jetties who were fishing the inlet with bottom rigs baited with cut weakfish belly. For days, that seemed to be the only bait the fish wanted. Fresh squid strips, shedder crab chunks, fresh fillets from snapper blues, and live baits would sit on the bottom without attracting as much as a sniff, while cut weakfish belly was quickly gobbled down by 5 to 9-pound weakies! Don't fight finicky fish—you'll come out a loser almost every time. Instead, give them what they want!

The favorite food of the moment can change in a hurry, such as from day to day, or even tide to tide. Shedder crab may be the hot morning bait, while the afternoon tide may bring a weakfish hankering for only squid. Weaks and specks are primarily opportunistic feeders, and they take advantage of what's most available to them at that particular time. Always carry with you at least several different types of baits and lures and don't hesitate to change your tactics when the bite slows.

A number of factors control when, where and on what weakfish and speckled trout will feed. At times, these factors may seem agonizingly difficult to understand, or even beyond human comprehension. However, the fishermen who consistently catch the most fish day in and day out, season after season, are those that make the effort to develop and maintain well-detailed log books, and they spend a great deal of time carefully studying their past successes and failures. They pay close attention to what's going on in the water and all around them, and to the tidbits of information that other successful fishermen may be willing to pass along. They identify patterns as they may pertain to time of day, season, location, tide, current, water depth and temperature, prevalent bait and so forth. They leave as little as possible to chance, and instead apply themselves to better understanding exactly what make weakfish and speckled trout tick when it comes to their feeding habits.

Shedder Crabs

A very productive and popular weakfish and speckled trout bait is a chunk of blue crab that was about to shed its shell. They're called "shedder crabs" in New Jersey, New York and points north, while anglers in Delaware, Maryland, Virginia and throughout the Mid-

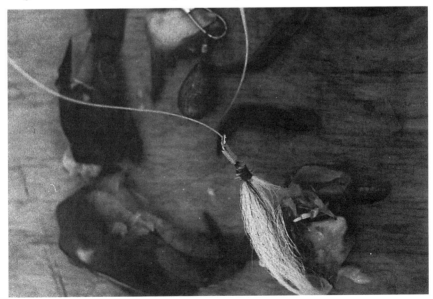

Shedder crabs are a tremendous weakfish bait, and can be used on bottom rigs, or to bring fish-attracting scent and flavor to bucktails and leadhead jigs.

Atlantic refer to them as "peeler crabs". Live shedder crabs can be purchased at many tackle shops. While they can be somewhat expensive at about $1.25 to $1.50 apiece, an individual crab can provide a number of trout-tempting baits.

The first step in the bait preparation process is to carefully handle the belligerent blue crab, with a goal of not getting pinched if at all possible. Pull off or cut off the claws, and save the claws as inside is a juicy piece of meat that makes a great bait. The next step is to hold the crab so that one hand is on top of the crab's shell, and the thumb on that hand is placed directly under a point on either side of the crab's shell. Use that thumb to lift straight up on the point of the crab - the whole back shell on a shedder crab will lift off with just a little pressure. Underneath will be a soft, tissue-like shell that is the same color as the outer shell that was just removed, and the soft shell would have eventually hardened when the crab shed the original shell. Then, and with a knife or pair of scissors, cut the crab in half lengthwise from between the eyes to the back end of the crab; there will now be two halves and each half will have legs on one side of it. Pull off the legs, then cut the two crab halves into smaller chunks (most anglers will cut between each leg socket or knuckle where the legs had joined the body). Counting the two pieces of crab meat from each claw, and the two to three chunks that are obtained from each half of the crab, a single blue crab will provide six to eight pieces of tantalizing bait.

It doesn't take a very big piece of peeler to provide scrumptious scent and taste that weakfish and speckled trout find irresistible. Shedder crab chunks are fished on bottom rigs and bucktails. A crab chunk stays on the hook better when it is hooked through a leg socket or knuckle.

Squid

Probably the most widely-used bait among inshore fishermen up and down the Atlantic Coast is squid. And why not, as squid catches summer flounder, bluefish, stripers, croaker, sea bass and practically everything else on the near-shore grounds, including weaks and specks. When many of us were youngsters, squid was the very first bait we ever hung on a hook and tossed into saltwater, and now, as adults, many of us wouldn't consider leaving the dock or ramp without a good supply of squid on board.

It's bait in perhaps its simplest form - flat, white strips. But the versatility and fish-appeal packed into those plain white strips make it an indispensable weapon in the pursuit of weakfish, speckled trout and other species. Weakfish will whack a strip of squid when it's

A widely-used bait among inshore fishermen, squid works great at tempting weakfish when cut into strip baits.

fished alone on a bare hook. Squid strips are also used to bring a seductive wiggle, scent and flavor to artificials such as bucktails, leadheads with plastic tails, spoons and metal jigs.

I'd be surprised if there's a saltwater bait and tackle shop anywhere along the East Coast that doesn't sell squid. The key to buying squid is whenever possible, purchase the biggest squid you can and when it's cut for bait it should provide nice, thick, white strips. Avoid inferior squid that yield only small, thin, yellowed or discolored strips.

After thawing, pull off the squid's head and tentacles (save them for bait), and then run a knife into the open end of the squid body (mantle). Slice it open so that it lays flat. Then use the knife blade to scrape away the thin reddish membrane on the outside of the squid. The next step is to cut the squid into pennant-shaped strips that are about one-half-inch wide at the widest end and that are from four to eight inches long before tapering down to a point. Whether fishing squid on a bottom rig or adding it to the hook of a lure, hook the strip only once through the thick end (do not hook the squid more than once and do not ball it up on the hook). The rest of the strip should hang freely and flutter and attract fish as it moves through the water.

An early-season project for many anglers is to purchase and prepare enough squid for an entire year of fishing. The squid is frozen in separate packages, each of which contain a specific amount of squid strips (the strips are usually coated with Kosher salt before freezing). That way enough squid can be taken on each trip without carrying along a bunch of extra squid that would not be used. If there are a few strips left over at the end of the day they are discarded (there is still plenty of squid at home in the freezer for upcoming trips). This prevents squid from being taken on trips, thawed out but not used, and then taken home and refrozen several times before ever being used. While it's not necessary to prepare an entire season's worth of squid ahead of time, it is a good idea to at least purchase and pre-pare squid a day or two before a planned fishing trip. That way, valu-able time on the water can be spent fishing instead of cutting bait.

Squid heads and tentacles also make good baits for bigger weak-fish and speckled trout. Just make sure that when they're hooked they move through the water without spinning or twisting. Bigger squid heads and tentacles, or even a whole squid, are often fished on a tandem-hook rig that prevents them from spinning.

In this world of high-tech lures, tackle and electronics, it's still tough to beat the fish-catching power of a plain old strip of white squid.

Chicken

In recent years, a rather surprising item has come out of nowhere to become an incredibly popular springtime weakfish bait, especial-ly in the Mid-Atlantic states of Delaware and Maryland. Until a few short years ago, this bait was never even found in a bait and tackle shop. And it wasn't something that could be caught in a cast net, or obtained from commercial watermen or purchased in a seafood store. In fact, it had nothing to do with fishing or the saltwater marine environment. This hot new bait is chicken. That's not a misprint, you read it right–chicken!

It's difficult to believe, but true. So many Mid-Atlantic fishermen have been using chicken for bait that many tackle shops all but had no choice but to find space in their bait coolers and freezers for the typical packaged chicken breast that is normally found in grocery stores. Instead of taking it home and frying it up for a delicious din-ner, anglers plop it in a cooler and keep it on ice until they arrive at the fishing grounds or surf fishing location. Then that white meat is cut into bait-size chunks that are simply hooked on standard bait rigs and lowered to the bottom, or hooked on surf rigs and cast out. Heads up and hang on, weakfish really do eat chicken! So do floun-der, bluefish and other species that make early-season appear-ances. But chicken's claim to fame in fishing is its ability to catch springtime weakfish. In fact, because it has proven itself to be just as productive, and maybe even more productive than shedder crabs, some tackle shop operators and anglers now refer to chicken as "Purdue Peelers".

Chicken is obviously not a natural part of the weakfish diet, and a number of theories have popped up as to why it is so effective. Some anglers say oil in chicken is released in the water and creates a fish-attracting sheen or scent trail that brings weakfish to the bait. When you consider that weakfish are famished after a long winter offshore, then it doesn't seem too surprising that they would devour any meaty pieces of chicken that they would come across, natural food source or not. Chicken probably made its first appearance on the fishing scene when an angler used it as a substitute for shedder crabs, which often are not available in bait and tackle shops until well after the early-season arrival of weakfish in April and early May. One must assume that some weakfish were caught, word began to spread, and then the rest, as they say, is history.

Strips of chicken breast have become very popular and productive baits among anglers in Delaware, New Jersey and Maryland, and are particularly effective on early-season weakies.

Grass Shrimp

Grass shrimp are a great bait for both weaks and specks, and they can also be used as chum to bring fish closer to the boat and into contact with your bait and hook. Grass shrimp can be purchased at many tackle shops, and an abundant supply can often be found hanging on dock and bridge pilings and also bulkheads. At the ramp, as I prep the boat and put it in the water, my young sons Cody and Ross enjoy rounding up a bunch of grass shrimp. They walk the dock and at each piling they stop and look down into the water. When grass shrimp are spotted on the pilings they simply lay on the dock and reach down and scoop them off the pilings with a small fine-mesh, long-handled net. Then the shrimp go into a small cooler where they are put on newspaper or a rag that has been laid on top of ice at the bottom of the cooler. Grass shrimp can be kept for future trips as they'll remain healthy and happy for quite some time when kept in the water in a live cart that features fine-mesh screening. They'll live longer when kept in water that has a current.

Live grass shrimp make the best bait and chum. However, weakfish and speckled trout can also be chummed in with frozen grass shrimp. When live grass shrimp are not readily available, frozen shrimp can be used as bait. Uncle Josh Freeze-Dried Grass Shrimp will also catch weaks and specks.

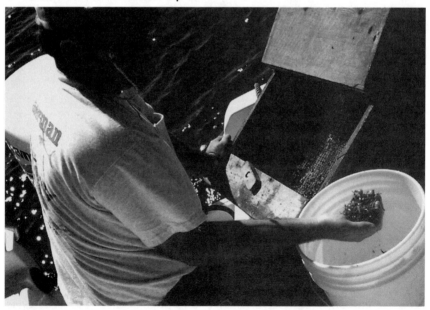

Grass shrimp are a great weakfish and speckled trout bait, and are especially effective when used as chum.

Chumming and fishing with grass shrimp are usually most productive from a boat anchored in shallow, back bay areas in depths of five to 25 feet. The beginning of an outgoing tide may feature an especially strong bite as fish will feed on grass shrimp and other small critters as they are flushed from the shallows and shoreline. Check a tide chart and try to arrange trips so much of the fishing time will be when the water is moving during an outgoing or incoming tide. Weakfish and speckled trout are most active during periods of moving water, and current will widely disperse chum and attract fish from great distances. The days and nights just before, during and immediately after a full or new moon are often very productive. The higher-than-normal tides will flood larger areas in back bays and outgoing tides will flush out plenty of shrimp and other fish food. Plus, the current is stronger, and the fish often more aggressive, during the full and new moon phases. Dawn, dusk and night are prime times as fish are more aggressive and boat traffic will be at a minimum.

Grass shrimping is no different than any other type of weakfish or speckled trout fishing in that structure plays an important role in where and how to fish. Don't just drop anchor anywhere. Look at a chart and study the water and surrounding shoreline to determine the exact location of any structure in the vicinity. Whenever possible, anchor in an area where the current will carry the chum and bait from shallow water, over a edge or drop-off and into deeper water. The important point is that it's crucial to fish structure of one form or another, as fish in back bay areas are usually found on, in and around holes, bumps, shoals, channels, hard bottom locations and the mouths of tidal rivers.

When chumming, occasionally toss over a small handful of grass shrimp. They should drift with the current some 20 to 40 feet from the boat, or should slowly sink out of sight, before another handful is tossed. It will be necessary to chum more quickly in a strong current, and more slowly in a weak current. Do not chum too quickly or with too many grass shrimp at one time as the fish will hang back and will fill up on the chum. Chumming shouldn't satisfy the fish, but instead should arouse their appetites and curiosity and should bring them closer to the boat where they'll run across the baited hooks.

It's very important to maintain a steady chum line. Any lapse in chumming will result in a break in the chum line that may prevent fish from following the chum all the way to the baits. It's easy to get distracted, especially when a fish has been hooked and the battle is on, but keep up the chumming. It's often a good idea to have a designated chummer who is charged with maintaining a steady chum line no matter what distractions may pop up. It's up to you to determine what the consequences should be if this person fails in the performance of his or her chumming duties, but in my opinion, a confiscation of their lunch and drinks, constant and merciless harassment, and solitary boat cleaning duties are the very least punishment that should be endured by anyone who may cause a good bite to go bad because they allowed a chum line to be interrupted.

Grass shrimp rigs are very simple. A size 1 Mustad 3176 Kahle hook, or size 1/0 or 2/0 Beak or Claw-style hook, is tied directly to the end of eight to 12-pound test monofilament line from the reel. If the reel is spooled with superbraided line, attach a mono leader to the superbraided line with an Albright knot, and then tie or snell the hook onto the end of the mono leader. Two, three or even four grass shrimp are threaded onto the hook, dropped overboard or gently lobbed-cast behind the boat, and allowed to drift with the current. Play out line so the bait can drift naturally with the chum. If the bait drifts well beyond the boat without a strike, then reel in, check the shrimp and replace if necessary, and start over.

Because many undersized weakfish may be released while grass shrimping, some anglers are switching over to circle hooks which tend to hook a fish in the corner of the mouth thereby making a quick release easy to accomplish. The corner of the jaw hook-up only occurs, however, if the fish turns away from the angler after taking the bait. It's the turn that makes the circle hook work. When weak-

Chumming with grass shrimp is typically done from a small boat anchored in eight to 25 feet of water in a back-bay area.

fish are aggressively taking baits and then swimming toward the boat, the circle hook will not work, and in fact, many fish will be gut hooked causing more damage than if a regular hook was used.

In a strong current, it may be necessary to add a small rubber-core sinker to the line well above the bait so it will sink a little in the water. Tom Pagliaroli is a well-known outdoor writer, press relations specialist at Wood Advertising in Ocean City, New Jersey, and an authority on light-tackle saltwater fishing. He uses a shad dart to effectively get grass shrimp down in a strong current. He fishes extremely light four to six-pound test line, and ties a shad dart directly to the line, and puts a shrimp or two on the shad dart hook. He recommends small chartreuse shad darts, or a chartreuse dart with a black head, or a chartreuse dart with a yellow head. Another tactic is to slip a one-eighth-ounce egg sinker on the line, then tie a small swivel onto the end of the line. An 18-inch piece of fluorocarbon leader, with a hook tied or snelled on the end, is then tied to the other end of the swivel. The swivel prevents the sinker from sliding down to the hook, and reduces line twist.

When the current is slow or not moving at all, and the bait has a tendency to sink quickly to the bottom, add a bobber to keep the shrimp suspended just off the bottom.

The often calm conditions, shallow water and aggressive fish found in back bays provide wonderful fly fishing opportunities. Weakfish working their way up a grass shrimp chum slick will often eagerly attack small Clouser minnows that fly fishermen drift and strip through the slicks.

Sea Worms

In some areas, sea worms don't seem to be used as much now for weakfish as they were years ago, yet weakies will eagerly gobble down sandworms and bloodworms. At low tide, some sea worms can be dug from the sand and mud on beaches and around jetties. They're also available in many tackle shops, and although they can be a bit pricey ($5 or $6 per dozen), most anglers appreciate the convenience and time-savings that come with purchasing worms instead of digging them up.

Greenish-colored sandworms and red bloodworms are especially effective on weakfish in the spring when fished in shallow-water near-shore locations that feature the warmest water and the most fish. They are also very productive when drifted along marsh banks and grassy shorelines in back bay areas and tidal rivers and creeks. Some anglers will very slowly troll worms along these banks and

Bloodworms and sandworms are very good weakfish baits and are popular among anglers fishing in the surf, back bays and tidal creeks.

shorelines to search out specific weakfish hot spots.

The tantalizing scent and flavor provided by sandworms and bloodworms will significantly enhance the appeal of weakfish bottom rigs and fish-finder rigs that are fished from boats, beaches, bridges, piers, docks and jetties. They are easier to hook, and will stay on the hook better, when they're threaded on thin-wire hooks. Insert the hook into the head end of the worm, and slide the worm along the hook shank until the hook point and bend can be exited from the worm while the head of the worm is at the eye of the hook. The worm should flutter enticingly from the hook; do not ball up the worm on the hook.

Bloodworms can also be used to produce other weakfish and speckled trout baits. In the summer and fall, bits of bloodworm fished on bottom panfish rigs with small hooks will catch spot, croaker and snapper blues. These fish can then be livelined, or filleted and cut into strip baits, for big weaks and specks.

While bloodworms and sandworms are somewhat expensive, leftover worms can be saved for future fishing trips by storing them in a refrigerator where they will stay alive for quite some time.

Mullet

Mullet are the magnet that draws hungry migrating predators close to our beaches each fall. Fishermen up and down the coast eagerly anticipate the fall mullet run and the spectacular fishing that it usually triggers. A big school of mullet is relatively easy to spot as those tightly-packed fish will appear as a dark cloud just under the surface of the water. At times, evidently when spooked or chased by bigger fish, hundreds of mullet in a school will suddenly, simultaneously and noisily erupt through the surface and out of the water. Anglers on jetties, piers, beaches and boats use a cast net to round-up their own mullet which are then fished live, or as fresh dead baits. Fresh fall mullet are also available by the bucketful in many tackle shops. While they're used primarily to catch bluefish, stripers and fluke, especially in the surf, mullet also work very well on weakfish and speckled trout.

Mullet can be filleted and the fillets are fished as strip baits. Whole dead mullet can be hooked through the eye sockets or up through the bottom of the lower jaw and out through the top of the head. Some anglers say it's important to scale whole dead mullet, or even fillet one side of them, as that allows more fish-attracting scent to escape from the bait and enter the water. Boating anglers fish whole mullet or fillets on a variety of standard bottom-fishing rigs. In the surf, mullet baits are often fished on a three-way swivel rig that has a colorful (red, orange, yellow or chartreuse) fireball just ahead of the hook that floats the bait just slightly off the bottom (and away from bait-stealing crabs). Surf rigs designed specifically for fishing whole mullet feature a fireball followed by a short piece of stiff wire that has a small loop on the end. The loop-end of the wire is pushed into the mouth of a dead mullet, pushed through the fish, and brought out the anal vent. Then a specially-designed double hook that is sold with the rig is slipped onto the loop.

Live mullet are most often hooked near the tail, dorsal fin or through the lips and fished on three-way swivel rigs or fish-finder rigs.

Mullet come in different sizes. It's finger mullet that hit the beaches and provide great bait each autumn from New England down through the Mid-Atlantic. Farther south, mullet get considerably larger than finger-size. While fishing for speckled trout, tarpon, snook and redfish in Sarasota, Florida, with Captains Rick Grassett and Merrily Dunn, I have seen, and heard, huge "corn-cob" mullet skyrocket out of the water and splash down in a manner that makes it easy to mistake them for a 5-pound bluefish or Spanish mackerel.

A standard whole, dead mullet bottom rig, effective for targeting weakfish in the surf.

Sand Fleas

A very good bait when surf fishing for weakfish can be found right at your feet, or at least under them. Sand fleas, also known as mole crabs and sand bugs, make tasty meals for weakfish. I have been on Mid-Atlantic ocean beaches in the summer and fall that have been absolutely polluted with these little gray creatures. Thousands and thousands of tumbling bugs can be seen as they are swept back into the ocean by water running off the beach. The sand fleas rolling across the sand are often small, yet reaching down, digging up and quickly sifting through a handful of wet sand will produce several big, fat fleas. This is a great source of bait that is free, abundant and easy to obtain. In fact, I often have all of the sand fleas I want without ever bending over to dig in the sand. My young sons have a blast making the sand fly and uncovering fleas. In five to 10 minutes they provide me with more fleas than I could possibly ever use in an entire day of surf fishing. Cody and Ross have also discovered that a single little sand flea can provide lots of entertainment beyond catching fish. They sneak up and quietly and carefully place a sand flea on Mom's shoulder, arm or leg as she peacefully naps in a beach chair. Then it's just a matter of standing back and enjoying the show as Mom feels the flea, sees the flea crawling on her skin, and goes absolutely ballistic.

Sand fleas may not be quite so abundant on some beaches, and in some areas they can be difficult to locate and catch. They are also available for purchase at many bait and tackle shops.

Sand fleas will survive all day (and then some) in a little wet sand at the bottom of a bucket or bait cooler. Just be sure that at the end of the day, when releasing unused sand fleas, that every last flea is given its freedom. It's absolutely amazing how a single sand flea, left to dry out in a closed cooler, can create such a horrific eye-watering, hair-curling stench. I was once practically knocked over after opening a cooler that contained nothing but one dead sand flea. I rapidly slammed the lid closed and dragged the cooler out of the garage and sprayed out the sand flea carcass with a garden hose - there was no way in the world I was going to touch that thing! Days after that memorable episode, I could still detect the smell of the sand flea in the garage.

Sand fleas are hooked by entering the hook point in the bottom (belly side) of the flea and out through the outer shell. Use a long-shank hook and slide on two, three or even four sand fleas at a time (depending on their size). For weakfish, sand fleas are used primarily by surf fishermen, who fish them on standard surf rigs, or on a rig that's weighted with only a very small sliding egg sinker that is put on the main line ahead of a swivel that attaches a two-foot leader and hook to the main line. The swivel prevents the sinker from sliding down to the hook and bait. This lightly-weighted rig will roll around in the water and provide the bait with the natural appearance of a sand flea that's being swept along as waves move up on the beach, and as water recedes off the beach.

While sand fleas are used more frequently to catch blackfish (tautog), stripers and pompano, weakfish anglers on the beach should never overlook this productive bait that's often readily available right at their feet.

Live Baits: Spot, Croaker, Snapper Blues, Bunker

Live bait, swimming and struggling on a hook, was especially devastating on the big tiderunner weakfish that were so abundant in the 1970s and early 1980s. Beginning in the mid to late 1980s and continuing through the early 1990s, live bait became obsolete simply because there were precious few big weakfish around to eat them. But now, as the weakfish comeback continues, and more and more trophy fish become available each season, these baits are again gaining favor among weakfish enthusiasts.

The key to using live baits to capture big weakfish is to fish them where the big fish are. Drifting a lively snapper bluefish over the shoals in the daytime during the summer may turn up a doormat fluke, but when it comes to weakfish the result will only be empty coolers and wasted time. After the early-spring run of weakfish up the coast and inshore, the largest weaks then head for heavy cover, including bridge pilings, wrecks, lighthouse boulders and other rock-piles. These are the locations where anglers can realistically expect to take trophy tiderunners on live bait.

For many anglers, especially in the Mid-Atlantic and south, Norfolk spot is the undisputed champion of live weakfish baits. These bottom-feeding palm-size fish can be best caught in the summer and early fall on bottom-fishing rigs with small hooks baited with a bit of bloodworm. Another live bait that tempts weakfish is the Atlantic croaker, also known in some areas as hardhead. It can be difficult not to catch croaker in the summer and fall when they're plentiful in Delaware, southern New Jersey, Maryland and Virginia. They attack bloodworm, squid, peeler crab and various cut baits, and they're often hauled up two at a time. In fact, anglers after flounder and other species often curse croaker because they jump all over baits the instant they hit bottom, thus denying other fish the opportunity to find and eat the baits. Spot and croaker are delicious and it's a good idea to take home for dinner a couple of the bigger specimens that are caught.

Something that would surprise fishermen in New Jersey, New York and New England is that many Mid-Atlantic anglers do not use live snapper bluefish for bait. As northern anglers will quickly confirm, snappers are great bait for tiderunner weakfish, trophy summer flounder, stripers and slammer bluefish. Cobia, red drum and king mackerel will also chow down on snapper blues. Little bluefish can be caught on practically any kind of cut bait fished on a bottom rig, and also on small bucktails, spoons, plugs, flies and streamers that are cast and quickly retrieved or stripped.

While not commonly used for weakfish, anglers shouldn't overlook the opportunities live bunker and fresh cut bunker provide for putting big weakies in the cooler. Bunker are also known as menhaden, pogy, fatbacks and alewives, and schools of this oily fish can be seen splashing and flashing across the surface of the water during the summer and fall months. On a few rare occasions, bunker will bite a baited hook or lure. But since they are easily seen on the surface, the most common and practical ways of catching them include throwing a cast net over them, or snagging them by casting and quickly retrieving through them a bunker-snagger rig that features two or three treble hooks on a leader ahead of a two to four-ounce sinker. Dropper loops are tied in the leader to hold the treble hooks.

Live wells are a must for keeping live bait lively, and different setups are available for different size and style boats.

All of these baits will naturally swim toward the bottom when hooked and dropped into the water or cast to structure. They can be fished on a rig featuring nothing more than a swivel, a two to three-foot leader of 30 to 50-pound test mono, and a short-shank live bait hook in size 5/0 or larger. In a hard-running current, or to help get the bait down, a sliding egg sinker can be added to the main line ahead of the swivel (the swivel separates the sinker and bait and prevents the sinker from sliding down the leader to the bait). Live baits are often hooked in the back, either ahead of or just behind the dorsal fin. You'll want a live bait that swims and provides lots of action, but sometimes bluefish and other live baits can be just too frisky or speedy. They can be slowed down by using a knife to cut off the bottom half of their tail.

Live baits can be lob-cast toward rockpiles, bridge pilings and jetties, dropped down to wrecks, or even drifted behind a boat. When extra weight is suddenly detected on the line, or when a big weakfish or speckled trout begins to move off with the bait, resist the urge to immediately set the hook. With live bait, a drop-back is needed to ensure the weakie or speck has the bait well inside its mouth. When fishing with spinning tackle I'll hold the rod tip high as the bait swims around, and as soon as a pickup is detected I'll provide the drop-back by quickly lowering the rod tip. If needed, I'll then open the bail to let out even more line. As I'm doing this I'll count to five, then it's time to close the bail and set the hook hard with a rapid and firm raising of the rod tip. With conventional tackle, I leave the reel's spool disengaged and use my thumb to control the line. I'll raise my thumb and allow line to slowly come off the reel as the bait swims. I'll prevent backlashes by pushing down with my thumb and applying pressure to the spool as needed. When a strike or pickup is detected, I'll lift my thumb to let out line, count to at least five, engage the spool, lower the rod tip, carefully reel in all slack, and then set the hook with authority!

Countless trophy weakfish are caught each season on live baits such as spot, croaker and snapper bluefish.

Other Baits

After the springtime spawn, bigger weakfish of about 5 pounds and up head for heavy structure such as lighthouse rocks and wrecks. Meanwhile, smaller 12-inch to 4-pound weaks spread out and spend the summer months on shoals, sloughs, edges and other bottom contours that also attract and hold fluke (summer flounder). Anglers targeting flounder will drift that structure with mummichogs, killies, shiners and minnows, which are not typically used for weakfish and speckled trout bait. However, in keeping with their predatory nature, weaks will gobble down minnows when the opportunity presents itself. In fact, many weakfish each season make their way into the coolers of flounder fishermen because they could not resist minnows on bottom rigs intended for flounder. On the other hand, fishermen in pursuit of weakfish usually bait up with shedder crab, squid, chicken and other cut baits.

Live eels are another bait that aren't normally used for weakfish, but manage to catch weakfish anyway. Most of the weakies taken

While live eels are most often used for striped bass, they'll also catch weakfish, particularly when fished around jetties, lighthouse rocks, and bridge pilings.

on eels are hooked by anglers on jetties, and anglers in boats, who lob live eels near jetty rocks in hopes of coaxing strikes from stripers. Eels elicit the most strikes, from both stripers and weakfish, in the darkness of night, and during the low-light periods of early morning and late evening.

Cut mackerel, especially flashy white strips cut from the belly section of the mackerel, provide an oily, scent-packed highly-visible bait. It's primarily drifted on bottom rigs, or fished in the surf, for bluefish, stripers and flounder. However, weakfish will also munch on mackerel. It's a great bait in the spring as Atlantic mackerel are migrating up the coast and fresh mackerel is available in many tackle shops. Mackerel can also be frozen and used as bait throughout the season.

Oils And Scents

Crab Imperial squid comes already cut into strips and marinated and frozen in peeler crab oil. That's a great combo - the wiggle and sight-appeal of squid combined with the scent and flavor of crab! These prepared baits are convenient (no cutting of squid required) and are very effective on weakfish and other species.

There are a number of oils available that fishermen can use to enhance the appeal of cut and fresh bait, and to bring scent and flavor to artificial lures. Liquid Frenzy, Baits Alive, peeler oil and bunker oil are a few of the oils and scents that are commonly available in many tackle shops. Just prior to casting, weakfish anglers will hang a bucktail, or soft plastic bait such as a worm or grub, or cut squid and other baits, over the side of the boat and squirt it with crab oil or

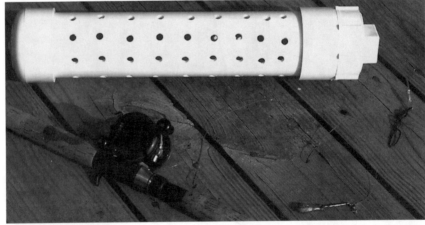

Fish scents and chum are a great way to further increase the fish-attracting qualities of natural and artificial baits alike. This chum tube is made from a length of PVC pipe.

fish oil. In the water, the oil creates a tantalizing trail of scent that helps attract fish directly to the bait or lure.

Instead of occasionally squirting oil on lures and baits, some anglers prefer to soak them in a container of oil for several hours, or even overnight. Some use a needle or hook point to poke small holes in soft plastic baits to enable the bait to better soak up the oil. While this obviously builds up a concentration of oil on each bait or lure, care must be taken not to over do it with some artificials. For example, soft plastic baits that are allowed to soak too long in fish oil or crab oil can become hard and brittle. The need to soak soft plastic baits in fish and crab oil has diminished in recent years with the availability of Berkley Power Baits and other soft plastics with built-in scent and flavor, and salt impregnation. Yet these oils remain a great way to bring even more fish-attracting scent and flavor to bucktails, squid and other artificial and natural baits.

Crab oils and fish oils can also be used to spice up a chum slick. I have fished with anglers who will occasionally pour some oil directly onto the surface of the water so the current will carry it with the chum that is being dispersed through the water.

Chapter Five

FISHING WITH LURES

Every day fish eat other fish, crabs and worms made of scales, flesh and blood. That's why the live and cut baits described in the previous chapter are so effective. However, using our fishing skills to deceive fish to the point where they'll open up and attempt to eat a chunk of lead dressed with deer hair, or a piece of hard or soft plastic, or other materials not naturally found in the marine environment, is another story altogether. Fish will consume a wide variety of fish, worms and crustaceans, yet they can be mighty particular about exactly what they'll eat at any given time. To be consistently successful with artificial lures, anglers must thoroughly understand their quarry and its favorite foods and feeding conditions. They must possess casting accuracy and the expertise required to present lures to fish in a manner that makes them look natural and alive. Fishing with artificial lures is challenging, fun and very rewarding.

From small skinny worms to big chunky bunker, the boatload of soft plastics now available feature spittin' images of practically everything that weakfish and speckled trout love to eat. They can be rigged and fished in an incredible variety of ways that make them swim, crawl, dance, dart and hop just like real baitfish, worms and crustaceans. Not only do they look and move just like the real McCoy, many soft plastic baits are impregnated with chemicals that also make them smell and taste like the marine critters they are designed to imitate. They are lifelike in every detail, and a valuable tool in every fisherman's arsenal.

While technology has brought us plugs and plastics that feature fantastically lifelike finishes, swimming action, scent and even flavor, it's still up to the angler to fish them correctly and in the right spots at the right times. Plugs will provoke strikes from weakfish and speckled trout in many different locations and situations, from trolling them in deep water to casting them up and under docks and mangrove roots in very shallow water. For a great number of anglers, casting and working plugs is the most exciting way of fishing for trout, both weaks and specks. Of the dozens of tactics and techniques that can be used to catch weaks and specks, I consider jigging to be perhaps the most enjoyable and productive. It's tough to top the versatility of bucktails as they can be trolled, jigged on the bottom, and cast around structure and in the surf. Bucktails have been so popular for so long that they've probably caught more weakfish than any other artificial lure.

When it comes to color selection for plugs, bucktails and other artificials, the traditional recommendation of using dark colors (black, brown, purple) at night and on overcast days, and light colors (white, yellow, chartreuse) on bright days, is still probably the most practical advice that can be given. And as will be mentioned several more times throughout this chapter, the size and profile of a lure also deserve very careful consideration.

The Power Of Plastics

Soft plastics are in no way new to the saltwater fishing scene, but today's baits are light years ahead of the straight plastic worms our parents and grandparents used to catch fish in both fresh and saltwater. Over the years, those early worms were eventually enhanced with developments such as the curly tail, and built-in flavors including grape and raspberry. Some fishermen considered it odd that weakfish, speckled trout and other fish would have a hankering for fruit and berries, while others said the real benefit the tastes provided was that they covered human scent that was on the bait after it was handled by the angler. No matter, they caught plenty of fish and triggered an explosion in the development of new, exciting, technologically-advanced soft plastic baits that continues to this day.

Soft plastic worms, shad bodies and any other of the numerous shapes and designs that are available, can be fished from the surface of the water down to the very bottom, and everywhere in between. To work them on or near the top of the water, simply thread them onto a hook that has been tied to the end of the line. Cast and retrieve this weightless offering; twitching the rod tip which will make the plastic dive and dart in an enticing manner practically identical to that of an injured, struggling baitfish. This is a productive presentation for weakfish and speckled trout in shallow and relatively calm water, especially in the mornings, evenings and at night. Put a plastic bait on a lightweight leadhead and it can be cast and allowed

A brace of weakfish that fell for a lifelike soft, plastic-tail fished on a lead head jig. Tails come in a variety of colors, sizes - some even have fish scents.

to wash around in the current while slowly sinking near lighthouse rocks and other fish-holding structure. They can also be cast and reeled in slowly and steadily near bridge pilings, docks and piers, and over wrecks, artificial reefs, rockpiles and shoals. A heavier leadhead will carry a soft plastic bait to the bottom where it can be jigged to imitate a dying baitfish. Some baits will come to rest with the leadhead directly on the bottom while the lighter plastic bait sticks up, which looks like a baitfish feeding directly on the bottom. Bouncing a leadhead/plastic bait combo on the bottom can also kick up puffs of sand or mud, giving it the appearance of a crab or shrimp that is burrowing into or hopping along the bottom.

The realistic profile, motion and color, plus the lifelike scents and flavors that are built in many plastic baits, mean they'll catch fish naked - there is really no need to dress them up with live or cut bait. A soft plastic bait feels real, and a fish that grabs it will hold on a bit longer than it would with other less lifelike artificials, providing the angler with an extra second or two to set the hook. However, some anglers feel more confident when a leadhead/plastic tail combo is further enhanced with a piece of bait. If it's necessary for you to do this, use a thin strip of squid that's shorter than the plastic tail, or a very small piece of shrimp. Sometimes it's possible to get away with a tiny chunk of shedder crab. Just be sure the bait isn't too big - a large bait will foul the action of the soft plastic and detract from its effectiveness, not add to it.

Soft plastic baits can be used to bring extra fish appeal to bucktails and single-hook metal jigs. Put them on the hook so they'll flutter enticingly. They can also be hooked on a bottom rig, either alone, or along with a strip of squid or other cut bait.

Improvements have also been made to the leadheads that soft plastic baits are fished on. I've heard largemouth bass fishermen say they had their "pants pulled down" when they reeled in a soft plastic that a fish had struck and the plastic had been pulled off the leadhead and bunched up on the hook. Manufacturers have taken steps to combat this problem by developing leadheads and hooks that firmly hold plastics in place. Many leadheads now feature small baitholder barbs that enter the plastic as it is slid onto the hook and leadhead. Also available are hooks with specially-designed shanks (usually shanks with a bend or crook) that help keep plastics in their proper place. A trick that largemouth bass fishermen have used for years, that some saltwater anglers have been picking up on, is to dab a drop or two of quick-drying Super Glue or Crazy Glue on the nose of the plastic where it meets the leadhead.

However, sooner or later, a plastic bait will begin to slide down the hook. After this happens several times, or after the nose of the bait begins to crumble, the life of the bait can be extended by taking it off the leadhead, cutting off one or two inches of the nose end of the bait, and rethreading it onto the hook.

Berkley has long been a leader in soft, scented plastic baits. The company's scientists in Spirit Lake, Iowa, use Berkley's extensive laboratory, which includes a huge testing tank, to see firsthand how fish react to the lures, and the scent and flavor chemicals, they develop. I have watched as Berkley officials have demonstrated with live largemouth bass and other freshwater fish the effectiveness of plastics such as Power Baits and Sqwormers. I am here to tell you that fish aggressively grab them and tenaciously hang on.

Lunker City produces two extremely popular and productive plastic baits in the Fin-S Fish and Slug-Go. The long, slender Fin-S Fish has proven to be especially awesome on speckled trout, and it also works very well on weakfish. Lunker City also markets Hydro-Tail worms and grubs, and Muscle Worms.

Fishermen for years have been raving about the fish-catching power of Bass Assassins. One of the newer lures in that lineup is a Glass Shad that features a prism insert and silver specks that provide fish-attracting flash and sparkle.

D.O.A. Lures are very popular among southern anglers, especially

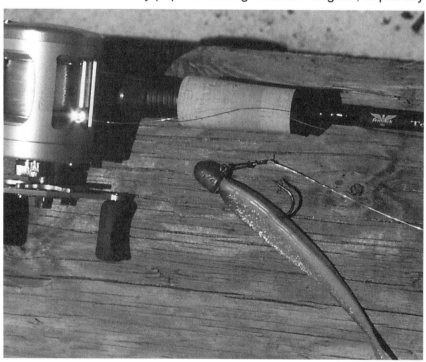

Soft plastics have been gaining in popularity among weakfish anglers as they offer a natural-looking bait and are available in countless color combinations.

in Florida, because they are so incredibly effective at provoking strikes from speckled trout, and also redfish, snook and tarpon. They have also done very well on weakfish and striped bass in more northern waters. These molded plastic baits come in sizes, body shapes and silhouettes that make them dead ringers for shrimp, crabs and minnows, and even larger forage such as bunker, butterfish and shad. Captain Rick Grassett at Snook Fin-Addict Charters in Sarasota, Florida, does very well on speckled trout with the D.O.A. TerrorEyz. It features a soft plastic molded body that completely wraps around the leadhead and hook, and it comes with large fish-attracting eyes. Cotee jigs and Slimy Slugs are other powerful plastic baits that speckled trout and weakfish often cannot resist.

The three-inch Swim Fin Grub from Riptide Saltwater Lures does a great job of imitating silversides, anchovies, spearing, sand eels, shrimp and other small baits that Mid-Atlantic and Northeast weaks and specks love so much.

Luhr-Jensen squid-bodied lures comes in sizes of 1/8 ounce all the way up to 24 ounces; the smaller sizes are very effective on weakfish and speckled trout.

For decades, a jar of Uncle Josh pork rind has been a faithful companion on each and every fishing trip made by many anglers up and down the coast. And why not, as the strips of pork rind bring

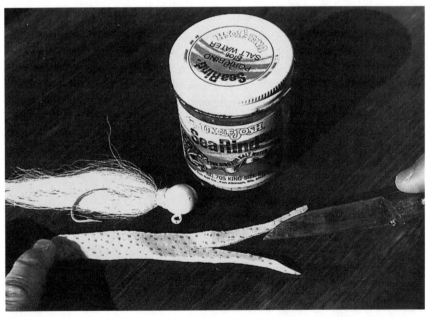

The addition of pork rind or plastic trailers can make jigs even more attractive.

strike-enticing flutter and scent to bucktails, leadheads, jigs and trolling lures. Now Uncle Josh makes available plastic worms and other soft baits that are impregnated with powerful pork scent.

Sassy Shad, Mr. Twister, Kalin's, Gene Larew soft plastics, Mr. Wiffle…the list of outstanding plastic baits is too numerous to detail. The purpose here is not to promote any specific bait, but to highlight the many technological advancements in plastic baits, and the many great choices anglers have when it comes to pursuing weakfish and speckled trout with plastics.

Bucktails

They're simple, versatile, and best of all they're amazingly effective on an incredible variety of fish. Bucktails are nothing more than a little lead, a dab or two of paint, and some deer hair, feathers or synthetic material. In this age of highly-innovative plugs with super realistic finishes and swimming action, and plastic baits impregnated with life-like scent and flavor chemicals, there are still very few lures that can match the day-in and day-out productiveness of bucktails. They can be cast and retrieved, trolled, jigged and fished in any number of ways that enable anglers to completely and

The ever-reliable bucktail has accounted for countless numbers of weakfish and speckled trout over the decades. A plastic tail makes them even more effective.

effectively cover the water column, all the way from the surface to the bottom. Bucktails trigger strikes when they're cast out and quickly cranked in through bluefish, Spanish mackerel and other aggressive predators as they devastate schools of baitfish on the surface. Allow a bucktail to sink, and slowly crawl it along the bottom, or bounce it up and down, and it'll be mighty tempting to fluke, stripers, weakfish and speckled trout. All of these species will readily attack a bucktail as it is slowly trolled on or near structure. In fact, there are very few saltwater species–or freshwater fish for that matter–that cannot be taken on a properly-presented bucktail.

Many anglers further enhance the fish appeal of bucktails by putting on the hook a strip of squid, pork rind or cut bait; a piece of bloodworm or small chunk of crab; or plastic worms or other curly-tail plastic lures. The vast majority of weakfish and speckled trout that are caught on bucktails are taken as the jig is fished slowly along the bottom. This is especially true for early-season weakfish that feed very deliberately in chilly springtime water.

A number of tactics can be used to slow the retrieve of the bucktail to ensure that the bucktail remains on or very near the bottom - right in the trout strike zone. In a drifting boat, cast the bucktail in the direction the boat is drifting. Allow the bucktail to sink to the bottom, reel in slack, and bounce the bucktail up and down by flicking the wrist to raise the rod tip, and then lower the rod tip and reel in slack. Then flick the wrist again and continue this process until the boat drifts well past the bucktail. At times it is possible to fish a bucktail on the backside of the drift, but at times the speed of the drifting boat will cause the bucktail to move too quickly to interest weakfish and specks.

Another tactic that often brings strikes is to cast the bucktail at a slight angle to the boat drift. At first, the retrieve will be at an angle to you, then as the boat continues to drift the bucktail will swing in an arc in regards to your position. This results in a considerable change in the bucktail's action and speed. At this point, the bucktail will probably begin to rise slightly up and off the bottom, and many times this will provoke strikes.

Flicking the wrist and/or raising the rod tip up and down during the retrieve will hop a bucktail along the bottom. This bucktail action would seem to imitate a feeding baitfish or crab, or a bait that has been injured and is about to die. Or, fish may also be attracted by the puff of sand or mud that the bucktail kicks up as it strikes bottom. Another effective retrieve tactic is to swing the rod horizontally at about waist level from in front of you to behind you. This raises the bucktail slightly off the bottom and moves it nearly parallel to the bottom, which evidently resembles a spooked or fleeing baitfish.

Another productive approach is a slow and steady retrieve around structure and over grass-beds. Small in-line sinkers are

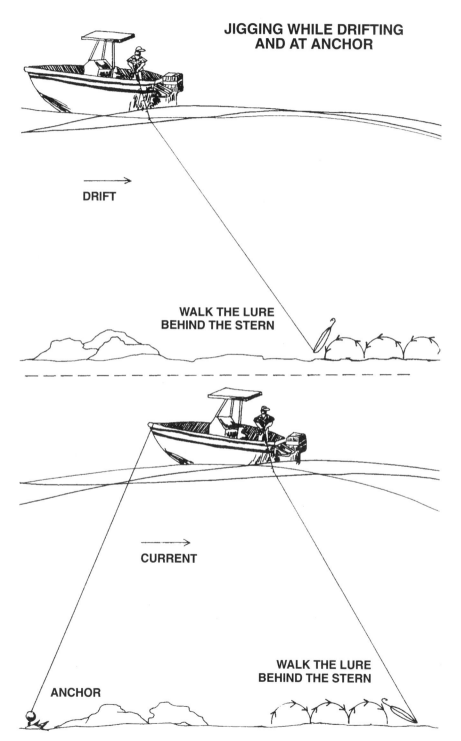

**JIGGING WHILE DRIFTING
AND AT ANCHOR**

DRIFT

WALK THE LURE
BEHIND THE STERN

CURRENT

WALK THE LURE
BEHIND THE STERN

ANCHOR

used by casting anglers to help get a bucktail down in a heavy current and/or deep water. The sinker is added to the rig about 18 inches to two feet ahead of the bucktail. The bucktail is tied on a two to three-foot piece of leader. A perfection knot is tied to create a loop in the other end of the leader. The loop is slipped through one eye of the in-sinker and over the sinker. The other eye on the sinker is snapped onto a snap swivel which is tied to the end of the line from the reel. This type of rigging, involving a snap swivel and a loop in the leader, makes it possible to quickly and easily change sinkers without cutting line and retying.

Spinning tackle and conventional tackle both offer their own unique advantages that every angler should consider when bucktailing. Spinning tackle is well suited for longer casts when tossing bucktails to fish and structure that are relatively far from the boat. However, the retrieve speeds on spinning reels are faster than on many conventional reels. With spinning tackle it can be difficult to retrieve a bucktail slowly enough to effectively crawl it along the bottom. On the other hand, the slower retrieve speeds of conventional reels are perfect for the low-and-slow bucktail presentations that work so well on weakfish and speckled trout.

The fishing line also plays a major role in determining how quickly a bucktail will sink and how long it will stay near the bottom. Thinner lines are subject to less water resistance than lines thicker in diameter–thinner lines cut through the water better and stay deeper longer than thicker lines. While some line strength may be sacrificed, fishing 12-pound test instead of 16 or 20-pound test (as an example) may make it possible to get the bucktail down to the fish. Superbraided lines are thinner in diameter than monofilament of comparable strength, and it's often much easier to keep a bucktail in contact with the bottom with superbraided line than it is with mono.

Trollers also use superbraided line, and wire line, to put bucktails right in front of bottom-feeding weaks and specks. Popular trout trolling rigs feature a three-way swivel; one eye of the swivel gets a mono dropper that holds a heavy sinker, while a monofilament leader with the bucktail is tied to the other swivel eye. Instead of a three-way swivel set-up, some trollers will rig an in-line sinker ahead of the leader and bucktail. Other options that enable anglers to troll bucktails down deep include planers and downriggers.

Surgical tube lures are very similar to bucktails in that they feature a head made of lead, or lead with an outer chrome finish. But unlike a bucktail, there's no deer hair on it. Instead, the head is adorned with a long, narrow tail made of surgical tubing that resembles an eel or worm. Usually very effective just as they are, it is possible to add a very small tidbit of shedder crab or squid strip for added attraction and flavor. Just make sure the bait isn't very big or it could cause the lure to spin during the retrieve.

In the first paragraph we discussed the simplicity of bucktails, yet they too can and have been improved with modern enhancements. Spro has applied to bucktails the 3-D technology commonly used on plugs and plastic baits. The result is a fishy-looking bucktail with a lifelike head that features laser eyes and hologram finish. Whether plain and simple, or new and improved, bucktails catch fish, and they're especially effective on weakfish and speckled trout.

Jigs And Metals

"Metals" is a term commonly used by anglers in some areas to refer to a broad number of spoons and jigs. These stainless steel or chrome-covered lead lures include, but are in no way limited to, Hopkins spoons, Crippled Herring jigs, Bass Pro Shops Strata spoons, Stingsilvers, Johnson Silver Minnow spoons, Acme Kastmaster spoons, Slim Jims, Jacky Jigs, jigs from Atom Manufacturing, Rapala Minnow Spoons and Rattle Snakie spoons—the list goes on and on. They're available in smooth or hammered finishes, lifelike holographic patterns, highly-reflective prism finishes, and with other fish-attracting enhancements.

Bottom-bouncing with Stingsilvers, Hopkins spoons, Jacky jigs, Crippled Herrings and other jigging lures is a very effective method for catching weakfish.

The narrow profiles of most metals result in very little air and water resistance, which means they can be cast a country mile, and they'll quickly cut through the water and settle to the bottom. Casting distance is an especially important feature for surfcasters when the wind is in their face, or when weaks and specks may be holding just off the beach and out of reach of bulkier, or lighter-weight lures. Metals also catch fish when cast to and from jetties and bridges and around lighthouse rocks.

Metal jigs and spoons are effective when fished just as they are. However, some anglers enhance them with cut bait. While not necessary, a single squid strip or other cut bait strip can be added to the hook. But a spoon or jig should not be baited with a piece of shedder (peeler) crab or other bulky bait because it may cause the lure to spin, or it may foul the lure's fluttering motion that weaks and specks and other species find so irresistible.

Many anglers replace the treble hooks on spoons and jigs with a single hook that has had the barb smashed down. This makes it much easier to unhook and release fish with very little damage to the fish, or angler.

Other productive jigging lures include Gotcha plugs, bucktails with a plastic worm or squid strip attached, and leadhead jigs dressed with plastics such as Sassy Shads, Bass Assassins, Fin-S Fish, Berkley Power Baits, Mr. Twisters, Kalin's, Cotee baits and other curly-tailed plastic worms.

All of these versatile and productive lures can be fished in a number of ways to tempt everything from aggressively-feeding fish to the most finicky of weakfish and speckled trout. When fish are actively chasing bait, metals can be cranked quickly across the surface to imitate panicked and fleeing baitfish. A slow and steady retrieve resembles a baitfish swimming normally. Perhaps most effective on weaks and specks is bouncing jigs and spoons along the bottom to give the appearance of an injured or dying baitfish, or a shrimp or a crab darting out of the sand or mud. Weakfish will whack them, and jigs fished in this manner will also provoke strikes from a number of other species, including stripers, bluefish, fluke (summer flounder), cobia, croaker (hardhead), sea bass, and yes, even skates and dogfish.

Weakfish and speckled jigging is a perfect application for super-braided lines. The no-stretch characteristics and increased sensitivity provided by Berkley Fire Line, Bass Pro Shops' Nitro line, Spiderwire, Western Filament T.U.F lines and others make them an ideal choice for jigging up weakfish and speckled trout. Some of the super-sensitive monofilament lines, such as Berkley Sensithin and Stren Sensor line, are also great lines to use for jigging. They make it very easy to detect strikes. The no-stretch feature provides for better hooksets, and because superbraided lines are thin there is very little water resis-

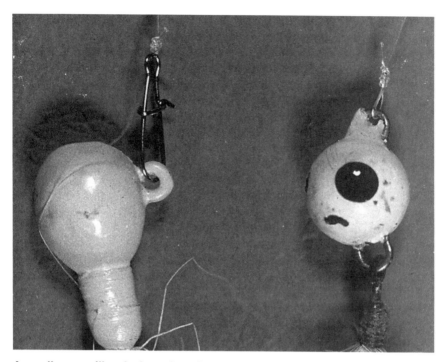

A small snap will make lure changing quicker, but sharp-eyed weakfish sometimes strike best when the leader is tied direct to the bucktail or lure.

tance for a more natural lure presentation. The increased sensitivity of
superbraided lines makes it easy for the angler to detect when the lure
has hit bottom. In fact, these braided lines are so sensitive that many
anglers can determine if the bottom is sand, mud, shell or rock, just
by the feel of the lure hitting the bottom.

Because these lines are considerably thinner in diameter compared to monofilament of the same strength, and because they are
also more expensive than monofilament, many anglers first spool their
reels about two-thirds full with mono, then use an Albright knot to
attach the mono line to a superbraided line which is then added to the
spool until it's full. A jigging lure can be tied directly to the end of the
braided line with a Palomar knot. However, many anglers prefer to add
a short shot (2 to 3 feet) of monofilament leader between the
superbraided line and the lure. The mono leader is attached to the
braided line either with an Albright knot, or via a small swivel between
the braided line and monofilament leader. Use a Palomar knot when
attaching the braided line to the swivel; a Palomar or improved clinch
can be used to tie the mono leader to the swivel.

Jig with a spoon or jig that's heavy enough to reach bottom but
isn't so heavy that it can't be effectively jigged. In shallow water, jigs
of one-quarter-ounce to one-ounce are usually more than sufficient.

In areas of deeper water and/or strong current, one-ounce to four-ounce jigs may be required to hit bottom. In a drifting boat, lower the lure to the bottom, take up any slack, and bounce it by raising and lowering the rod tip. The metal should be dropped to the bottom on a taut line so strikes can be detected as the lure flutters downward, and so the angler can also feel the "thump" of the lure hitting bottom (when contact with the bottom is lost, simply play out enough line to get the lure back down in the strike zone).

When jigging, or when using any artificial lure for any species, I believe lure size is the key to success. While lure color, shape and other details always deserve consideration, it is size that more often than not makes the difference between catching a limit or starving for a bite.

At night, on lighted piers, docks and bridges, I have seen weakfish dash toward the surface and devour minnows that had been attracted to the lights. These weakies are often hooked by anglers fishing shad darts, speck rigs and small, soft plastic lures on one-eighth-ounce and one-quarter-ounce leadheads, while bigger lures such as 1-ounce bucktails with a 6-inch plastic worm are usually ignored in this scenario. Weakfish will often key into size—when feeding on small bait they will only be interested in small artificials that closely match the size of the bait. The baitfish that weakfish (and stripers, bluefish and fluke) commonly feed upon are small, so I favor small spoons and jigs.

Yet there is more to the equation than just size. The jig will need to be heavy enough to drop through the water and hit bottom, and remain near the bottom as the boat drifts. That brings up appealing characteristics that the Hopkins Shorty, Stingsilver, Strata spoon and Crippled Herring all share: they are relatively heavy for their small size, and/or they feature narrow profiles that enable them to cut through the current and quickly hit bottom.

The addition of a teaser often greatly improves the effectiveness of a jigging rig. A wide variety of small artificials can be used as teasers, including flies and streamers, shad darts and small buck-tails, and lightweight (1/8-ounce to 1/4-ounce) leadheads dressed with plastic tails such as any number of small Berkley Power Baits, Sassy Shads, Bass Assassins, Mister Twisters and others. Teasers and their extra motion do more than just attract fish to the bigger jig, they also provoke strikes of their own. In fact, when bottom bouncing with a jig and teaser, many anglers are often surprised to hook up with a strong fish only to discover at the end of the battle that the big fish had overlooked the larger jig and had instead attempted to eat the smaller teaser. A word of caution is in order: When a fish hooked on either the jig or teaser is about to be boated or beached, it is important for everyone in the vicinity to remember that the rig features two hooks, and a flopping fish can send the bare hook flailing about in a potentially dangerous manner. If the fish is netted, the bare hook can foul in the net and removing the hook and untangling the mess can consume valuable fishing time.

Teasers can be added to jigging rigs in several ways. Probably the simplest and easiest approach involves tying a small dropper loop in the mono leader about two to three feet above the jig at the end of the line. The dropper loop can be pinched down and passed through the eye of the teaser and drawn tight. Or, by cutting one leg of the loop next to the dropper knot, the dropper loop can be changed into a single piece of line that stands off from the leader; the teaser is tied to the end of this line. Changing or removing the teaser is much easier when using the first method of slipping the teaser on and off the dropper loop.

When the boat is properly positioned to drift over a shoal, slough or other fish-attracting structure, the angler flips the lever or pushes the button to disengage the spool on light conventional or baitcasting tackle, or flips open the bail on a spinning reel, and allows the jigging rig to drop straight to the bottom. With spinning tackle the bail is then closed, while with conventional or baitcasting tackle the angler stops more line from coming off the reel by simply pressing down on the spool with his thumb. Gently lifting the rod 2 to 3 feet, and then lowering it again to the original starting point (about waist level), will impart an effective jigging motion to the rig. On the drop, the angler should be able to detect the jig coming into contact or "thumping" on the bottom. When contact with the bottom is lost, anglers with con-

Working the rod tip in an up and down motion enhances the action of a bucktail or plastic-tail lead head jig.

ventional or baitcasting tackle lift up on their thumb to play out more line, while spinning anglers open the bail, let out more line, and then close the bail again. The key is to keep the offering in the weakfish strike zone which is usually on or very near the bottom. After additional line is played out several times, the rig will eventually be too far from the boat to control and fish effectively. Anglers then reel in, drop down and start the jigging process over again.

Jigging can also be very productive from an anchored boat. Instead of dropping straight down as is done when drifting, anglers anchored on productive structure cast out, allow the rig to sink to the bottom, then retrieve it by slowly reeling in line and frequently twitching the rod tip.

It's important to pay attention during the entire jigging process as many strikes will come as the jigging lure falls back to the bottom; the fluttering motion and flash imitate a dying baitfish. A hard or dramatic hookset is not required with superbraided lines as their no-stretch characteristic will only cause the hook to be ripped out of and away from the fish. Instead, a short upward jab of the rod and immediate reeling will effectively drive the hook into the fish's mouth.

Jigging is especially effective in breaking fish under working birds. Often, small bluefish or stripers will chase bait to the top, while larger and more wary weakfish (and stripers) will hug the bottom under attacking bluefish, where they feed on scraps and wounded baitfish that fall from the melee on the surface. A jigging lure cast into the breaking fish will hopefully sink fast enough to get through the marauding bluefish. To the weakfish below it will appear to be a dying baitfish falling to the bottom. If it hits bottom without a pickup, the angler should jig or twitch the jigging lure once or twice and be prepared for a weakfish to whack it.

Plugs And Swimming Lures

Rat-L-Traps, MirrOlures, Halco Tremblers, Bombers, Rapalas, Cordell, Storm and Yo-Zuri plugs, the list goes on and on. Today's anglers are very fortunate to have at their disposal an incredible variety of plugs that look, swim and even sound like real baitfish. Plugs come in scores of dazzling colors and oodles of life-like finishes, plus they feature fish-attracting noise makers and realistic swimming actions. Noisy Rat-L-Traps swim with a lifelike tight wiggle, and they have long been extremely popular among weakfish and speckled trout anglers, especially those working the surf, back bays and along bridges and docks, especially at night. Any discussion of realistic-looking plugs has to include the Yo-Zuri. The Crank

N Shad features a strip of prism tape inside the lure for a super-reflective finish, plus its 3-D eyes and stainless steel rattling balls transmit sound and help maximize casting distance. There are floating, sinking and suspending versions of the Crystal Minnow that feature the Yo-Zuri holographic finish and seductive action. These are only a few examples of plugs that do an excellent job of imitating real baitfish, down to the very last detail.

As with jigs and other artificials, I believe the most important consideration is the size of the plug - always make it a point to use plugs in sizes that come closest to matching the size of the prevalent baitfish. A common mistake among many anglers is fishing plugs that are much bigger than the bait the fish are feeding on at that time. While there are always exceptions, it is safe to say that plugs and lures of four to six inches in length are usually the most productive on weakfish and speckled trout.

Another crucial factor when fishing with plugs is the speed of the retrieve. Slow is good, slower is better. While weakfish and speckled trout are aggressive predators, they aren't likely to chase a fast-swimming bait the way bluefish and Spanish mackerel will. Weaks and specks ambush their prey instead of running it down. A good goal for anglers to set for themselves is to turn the reel handle as slowly as possible (as long as the retrieve still imparts the proper action in the lure). Fishing plugs is much more than just a matter of

Many of today's plugs feature incredibly realistic finishes and swimming actions, and are available in floating, sinking and suspending models for all conditions.

casting and cranking. It may be necessary to experiment. Start slowly, and if strikes are few and far between, then increase the speed of the retrieve, but only a little at a time.

The reel obviously plays a huge role in the speed of the retrieve. A vast majority of today's spinning reels feature gear ratios of 5 to 1, even 6 to 1. It can be very difficult to turn the reel handle slowly enough to compensate for the fast retrieve ratio of such a reel. A slow retrieve is much easier to obtain with conventional or baitcasting reels that have gear ratios of about 3.5 to 1.

A slow retrieve is recommended, and there are some situations in which weakfish and speckled trout will actually respond to no retrieve at all. While wearing Korker sandals (with spikes on the bottom) for reasonably safe footing, and fishing from the jetties at Delaware's Indian River Inlet, I have cast sinking MirrOlures (usually black) upcurrent, but instead of retrieving them I have just kept slack out of the line and allowed the current to sweep the plug along in the inlet. Simply being pushed by the current has provided the MirrOlures with enough action to trigger strikes from both weaks and specks.

MirrOlures come through the water straight and with very little action, however, most plugs feature a side-to-side wobble or swimming motion. Some plugs come in floating and sinking models. The length and size of the lip on the plug will also determine how deep

Bombers, Windcheaters and Yo-Zuri lures are but a few of the plugs that will trigger strikes from weakfish and speckled trout.

the plug will dive on the retrieve or while being trolled. A bigger, wider lip "bites" into the water more and gets the plug deeper, and they are favored when fishing deeper water, especially in the day-time when weaks tend to stay deep. Plugs with shorter lips may be more productive at night, and in the evenings and early mornings, when weakfish and speckled trout will feed in shallower water and higher in the water column.

Plugs can be tied directly to the line with an improved clinch knot, or they can be connected to the line via a snap swivel. At times, a plug will noticeably run off to the right or left instead of swimming straight or true on the retrieve. This can be remedied by using pliers to gently turn the front eyelet on the plug in the direction the lure has been veering.

Plugs are used to effectively probe structure such as lighthouse rocks, jetties and bridge pilings. It's usually very important to cast right to the point where the structure meets the water. Plugs that are cast three or four feet short of the rocks may be eaten by bluefish, but weaks and specks will often ignore them. Casts that travel a bit too far may result in cracked plugs that collide with the hard structure. Casting accuracy is crucial and the goal is to put plugs right on the structure where the fish are holding.

Plugs also catch weaks and specks in the surf, and from piers and docks. MirrOlures are tremendously popular for speckled trout among Outer Banks surf fishermen in North Carolina.

I now often use a superbraided line (Berkley Fire Line, Spider Wire, Nitro line, T.U.F. lines) when plugging for weakfish and speck-led trout, whether it be from a boat, jetty, pier or beach. The thin diameter of those lines creates less air resistance and provides for long casts. The line's no-stretch characteristics make it very easy to detect strikes. While a Palomar knot can be used to tie a plug direct-ly to the end of a superbraided line, I prefer to fish plugs on a monofilament leader and I use an Albright knot to connect the mono leader to the braided line. The narrow-profile Albright knot will easily pass through the rod guides and will not hinder casting.

Most plugs come armed with two sets of treble hooks, some plugs even have three sets. To better protect the angler and others from unwanted piercing, to reduce the time and effort spent unhooking fish, and to lessen the stress and injury to the fish (especially fish to be released), some anglers remove the front set of treble hooks, and sometimes the middle set. Others will remove treble hooks from plugs and replace them with a single hook. Any change to the plug may affect its action so be sure to test it in the water before fishing with it.

Chapter Six

WHERE TO FIND WEAKS AND SPECKS

If there is one point that I would stress the most in this entire book, it is the extreme importance of identifying, locating and properly fishing structure. Structure is a term used to describe contours, changes and irregularities in the ocean bottom, and to a lesser degree in the water column. Structure of most interest to weakfish and speckled trout anglers include shoals (lumps or hills on the bottom), sloughs (valley-like depressions on the bottom), channels, wrecks, artificial reefs, jetties, lighthouse rockpiles, bridge pilings, shadow lines and sand bars.

Properly fishing structure requires an understanding of how fish relate to structure and the ability to apply that knowledge to various situations and conditions as they are encountered on the water. Anglers also need to understand tide and current and how water movement impacts fish and fishing on structure. Fishermen in boats need the electronics and equipment that will enable them to pinpoint the location of fish-holding structure so they can thoroughly fish it, and so they can return to it on future fishing trips.

I once heard the bottom of the ocean and bays compared to a desert in that a vast majority of it is flat, sandy, open areas. Just like a desert, the flat, sandy areas in the ocean and bays contain little or no life. In a desert, most of the life is found in an oasis, and in saltwater an oasis comes in the form of structure.

Perhaps just as important as structure are tide and current and the impact they have on the fish we want to catch. Let's begin this chapter with a discussion of tide and current, then we'll look at the various structure that attract and hold weakfish and speckled trout. This chapter is about shoals and sloughs, wrecks and reefs, and other structure that are accessed and fished in boats, in everything from 16-foot aluminum boats on up to big 26 to 31-foot fiberglass boats.

Tides And Current

Although some people use the words "tide" and "current" interchangeably, they are not the same thing. For example, at one time or another we've all heard someone say "The tide is running hard." That statement is not correct. It's the current, and not the tide, that "runs". Tide is the vertical, or up and down movement of water. Current is the horizontal, or sideways movement of water. So when someone says "The tide is running hard", what they actually mean is "The current is running hard".

Tides are created by the gravitational pull of the moon. The sun's gravity is also involved, but the moon has the most impact on tides because it's closer to the earth than the sun. On a rising or flooding tide, the current moves water into our bays and through our inlets, and on a falling or ebb tide the current moves out of the bays and inlets. At high tide the water is at its greatest vertical point, while at low tide the water is obviously at its lowest vertical point.

The moon rises just less than one hour later each day, so the same tidal stage at a particular location is about one hour later each day.

People sometimes confuse high tide or low tide with slack water. Some people mistakenly believe that at high tide all movement of the water will stop. But remember the difference between tide and current - at high tide the water will stop its vertical movement, but the current or horizontal movement of the water will continue for some time.

This is very noticeable in an inlet, and while wreck fishing. Visit an inlet at high tide and you'll notice that the current continues to move water from the ocean and into the inlet for some time after high tide. And while on a wreck at high tide you'll still have to contend with current as you attempt to get your baits down in the structure. The height of the water won't increase after high tide but the current will continue to move.

Eventually, the current will stop, and when that happens, that's what's known as slack water or dead water. It's at slack water when the water in the inlet stops (the current stops running), and when it gets much easier to fish straight up and down on a wreck. Slack water comes during high and low tides, but slack water begins well after the water has reached high and low tide. After slack water, the current will begin to run in the opposite direction as the tide begins to fall or rise.

Anglers need to be aware of tides and current because it's the movement of water that often triggers feeding activity among weakfish, speckled trout and other species. Generally speaking, the best fishing comes during times of moving water, and on the other hand the bite will slow and often stop during periods of slack water. Current is especially important on and around structure such as shoals, bridge pilings, jetties, channels, sloughs and drop-offs. As the current collides with the structure, or is interrupted or diverted by it, the water will swirl and tumble, and often carry along with it small baitfish, shrimp, seaworms and other forage. A strong current and structure create rips and eddies, which ring the dinner bell for weaks, specks, stripers, fluke, bluefish and other big, hungry fish. They realize moving water may stun, disorient and overwhelm baitfish, making them very vulnerable to predation.

In back bays, sounds and tidal rivers, incoming water and high tide provide weakfish and speckled trout with access to shallow water and near-shore locations. They'll move up to feed, especially during low-light conditions at night and during the evenings and early-morning hours. Outgoing water and low tide will usually confine fish to deeper water, but it often carries with it grass shrimp and

Weakfish are more active and feed more aggressively during times of moving water, as the current stirs up and carries with it baitfish, eels, worms, sand fleas and other tasty morsels.

small baitfish that have been flushed from the shallows. Current can also kick-start a strong bite by bringing warmer or cooler water onto the beach or into an inlet and back bay area.

The phase of the moon has a big impact on the tides and current, and therefore the fish. Full and new moon periods can bring extremely high tides that enable baitfish and predators to move into areas that would typically be inaccessible during normal tidal conditions. Full and new moons also bring extremely low tides that may drain some shallow-water areas that usually provide good fishing opportunities during more normal tidal conditions. It can also be difficult to maintain contact with the bottom and to effectively fish the extra-strong currents associated with new and full moon periods.

Depending on the location, and the particular structure that you fish, the best action may be during incoming tide, or outgoing tide, or in a narrow time frame during a specific stage of the tide. The phase of the moon, weather conditions and other factors also play important roles in determining when and where the fish will feed. Time on the water (experience) and careful note keeping in a log book, paying attention to information passed along by other anglers, and reading the Fishing Reports Section in *The Fisherman* magazine will enable you to develop a comprehensive understanding of when and where the best bites can be expected in the areas you fish.

Rock piles and similar structures are hot spots for trophy-size weakfish, and are especially effective when a good current is running by them.

Tide Rips

A "rip" is an area with waves that are higher than surrounding waves, or an area of water that is noticeably rougher than the water around it. On a calm day, a rip may be an area of "nervous" water (small ripples) surrounded by flat seas. At other times rips may feature waves two and three feet higher than other nearby waves.

A rip on the surface of the water indicates a change in the contour of the bottom. Rips usually form over shoals or other types of lumps and bumps on the bottom. In some bay and coastal areas the water depth may be generally 25 to 35 feet, but a shoal or lump may rise up and the water depth on top of the shoal can be 15 feet deep, or 10 feet, or even as shallow as five feet. In a moving current, the current collides with the shoal and water is forced up and over the structure. This causes the water to roll and tumble over the shoal or lump, creating a disturbance or rip on the surface. How rough the water is in a rip is determined by many factors, including the phase of the moon and strength of the current, the depth of the water around the structure and on top of it, and the wind. Rips can be very pronounced when the current is moving and will disappear as the current slows and eventually stops at the end of the tide.

In a moving current, when water tumbles over a shoal or lump, it carries along with it small baitfish, crabs and shrimp, which often become disoriented and are unable to swim against the force of the water. This makes them easy pickings for weakfish, speckled trout and other predators that can hold their own in the current, and this is what makes tidal rips such a great place to fish. Weaks and specks often hold on the downcurrent side of a shoal or lump and simply wait for the current to carry food over the structure and directly to them. Depending on the strength of the current and other factors, weaks and specks may position themselves in front of the shoal, or even on top of it, yet most often they'll hold on the downcurrent side.

Drifting is an effective way to thoroughly fish a rip and the structure below it. Position the boat upcurrent of the rip, drop down a baited bottom rig, and bounce it up, over and down the shoal or lump. Jigging from a drifting boat will also catch weaks and specks in the rips. Productive jigging lures include a bucktail dressed with a plastic worm or squid strip, a leadhead with a plastic tail, Hopkins spoons, Stingsilvers, Strata spoons and Crippled Herring jigs. These are bounced along the bottom as the boat drifts through the rip and over the fish-holding structure.

Speckled trout and weakfish will also whack a bucktail or leadhead with a plastic tail that is cast and retrieved from a boat drifting through a rip. It's important that the retrieve is slow and that the lure

FISHING THE RIPS

CURRENT

stays near the bottom. I've often had my best success while casting toward the rip while the boat is still upcurrent of the rip, and then slowly retrieving the lure through and away from the rip (the boat drifting toward the rip and the lure helps slow the retrieve). After the boat has drifted through the rip and beyond it, reel up and reposition for another drift. Never run straight through the rip as noise from the boat and motor will spook the fish and put off the bite. Instead, take the great circle route well around the rip when positioning the boat on the upcurrent side for another drift.

Trolling will also take fish from tidal rips. Troll parallel to the rip, just barely upcurrent of the rip, so the current will push the lure into the rip and onto the structure. Troll slowly to keep the bait near the bottom. Superbraided lines and wire line are commonly used by trollers as they cut through the water and get deep. In-line sinkers, three-way swivel rigs with sizable sinkers, and planers are used to get lures down deep. Trolling low and slow with bucktails, swimming plugs and spoons will provoke strikes from weakfish and speckled trout, and also striped bass, bluefish, fluke and other predators that are found in tidal rips.

Looking at a chart and studying the bottom contours will reveal shoals, lumps and other structure that will feature rips during a moving current. Sometimes the disturbed water in a rip can be heard

Productive lures for fishing rips include bucktails, leadheads with plastic trailers, and jigging spoons.

for considerable distances–keep your eyes and ears open to locate rips that hold big weaks and specks. Some rips are more productive during incoming tide, others during a falling tide, or the bite may be better at the beginning or end of a tide. Make note of this and other important points in a log book following each fishing trip, maintain an updated list of LORAN TDs or GPS coordinates of all good rips, and you'll be able to repeatedly return to and fish rips during their most productive periods.

Sloughs, Channels & Drop-offs

Sloughs and channels are like valleys or troughs on the bottom of the bay or ocean. They feature edges or drop-offs on both sides that fall from shallower water to deeper water at the bottom of the slough or channel. Some sloughs and channels are very pronounced with steep drop-offs and water that is considerably deeper than the surrounding water. Others can have gently sloping drop-offs and water that is only slightly deeper than the water around them. Sloughs and channels are found in areas of shallow water and deep water, they can be wide or narrow, long or short. Search them out on charts of the areas you fish, and get their LORAN TDs or lat/lon position. Channels and sloughs attract and hold weakfish and speckled trout and they are great places to jig, cast lures, bottom fish with bait, and troll.

It is the edges and deeper water that these structures provide that make them so attractive to baitfish, weakfish and speckled trout. Baitfish will bunch up and hold tight along the edges of sloughs and channels in attempts to hide from any nearby predators. Small baitfish are carried by the current from shallow water over the edge and down the drop-offs of channels and sloughs. At times, weaks and specks will hang tight to the edge and allow the water to practically push bait directly into their mouths. When the current collides with an edge the flow of water is often altered, which can create swirling water that can stun baitfish and sweep them along with the current. These are fantastic feeding conditions that weakfish and speckled trout will not pass up.

Just like baitfish, weaks and specks will at times hug drop-offs to avoid the jaws of chopper bluefish, cobia, inshore sharks and any other big hungry fish that may be around. Edges also provide fish with quick and easy access to both shallower and deeper water. When the sun is high in the sky during the day, light-sensitive weaks and specks will often stay in the deeper water near the bottom of sloughs and channels. Then, as the sun begins to go down in the evenings, they'll cruise up the edges to shallower water in search of food. Tides also need to be considered, as a falling tide generally

Weakfish and speckled trout will congregate in channels and sloughs, and trolling the edges of that structure with bucktails and plastics will often result in hook-ups.

confines fish to deeper water in channels and sloughs, while a rising tide enables them to move up and into nearby shallower water.

Especially productive locations are areas where a channel or slough may bend or curve. Look for these spots on charts, or get the LORAN coordinates or lat/lon when a bend or curve in a channel or slough is noticed on the fishfinder. These areas can be considered "structure within a structure" as the edge of a channel or slough is structure in itself, and then the curve or bend provides even more structure and fish appeal. Baitfish may seek out and hide along the edge right where a channel or slough curves, or they may be swept in and held there by swirling water in a strong current.

When conditions allow, a very effective drifting pattern for bait fishermen and jiggers begins in the shallower water near a channel or slough, and then carries the boat over the edge and along the drop-off and then into the deeper water over the bottom of the channel or slough. When possible, a natural presentation for anglers casting bucktails, leadheads with plastics, and live baits is to allow the current to push the offering down a drop-off toward the deeper water in a channel or slough. Sometimes the wind and/or current won't allow for the perfect drift or casting opportunities; the key is to drift over the drop-off and the deeper water one way or another for as long as possible, and as soon as the boat drifts beyond the productive structure it's time to reposition for another drift. Trollers can work a zig-zag pattern back and forth over the edge which pulls the lures both up and down the drop-off. Or they can troll parallel to the channel or slough to keep their lures constantly over the drop-off or in the deeper water. The first troll usually begins in the shallower water near the top of the drop-off, while each subsequent pass will be in slightly deeper water farther down the drop-off.

Sloughs are especially important structure for surf fishermen. These areas of deeper water are generally found a short distance off the beach, they generally run fairly parallel to the beach between the outer bar and beach, and predators like weakfish and speckled trout cruise up and down the sloughs and slurp down baitfish, crabs, sand fleas, shrimp and other tasty morsels. Because the water in sloughs is deeper than surrounding water, it's usually easy to see the darker-colored water in a slough. Many surf fishermen make the common mistake of casting too far - their lures and baits travel over and beyond the slough where the fish are. Sloughs along the beaches of North Carolina's Outer Banks are fantastic speckled trout fishing locations; anglers nail them on leadheads with plastic tails, speck rigs (two shad darts rigged in tandem), MirrOlures, bloodworms, peeler crab chunks, cut mullet and spot, and other lures and baits.

Lighthouses

Weakfish move up the coast and into our bays, sounds and tidal rivers in early spring. Then, in late spring and early summer, the bigger tiderunners head for heavy structure, both in the inshore waters and in the ocean. While great numbers of summertime anglers enjoy catching 13-inch to 3-pound weaks on shoals and sloughs, weakfish enthusiasts looking to tangle with tiderunners of 4 to 12 pounds concentrate their efforts on heavy structure including wrecks, rock-piles and lighthouses.

The rocky bases at lighthouses are fish magnets as they provide fish with both food and protection. Small forms of marine plant and animal life grow on and among the boulders, and baitfish, eels and crabs move in to feed on them. Weakfish, stripers, fluke and bluefish hit the rocks to devour the baitfish, eels and crabs. Lighthouse boulders bustle with life, similar to an oasis in the middle of the desert. These rocks are like restaurants, where fish come to eat.

An extremely effective method for fishing lighthouses, involving 11-inch plastic worms and a colorful assortment of Bass Assassin plastic lures on one-quarter-ounce to 1-ounce leadhead jigs, was demonstrated to me by Pete Dressler, a Maryland angler well-

Artificial lures and live baits fished on and around the rocky bases of lighthouses will produce nice catches of big weakfish.

known throughout the Mid-Atlantic region for his innovative and highly-productive fish-catching techniques. The presentation used with these plastic baits has been described as "floating worms," and it works wonders around heavy rock structure, especially the rocky bases at lighthouses. It's an approach that all anglers would find relatively easy to implement.

Precise anchoring and boat positioning are required to establish the casting angles needed to properly float the worms and Assassins to the fish. The idea is to anchor just off to one side of the lighthouse (not directly upcurrent or downcurrent of it). The best fishing comes during times of moving water, either incoming or outgoing tide.

Many anglers would consider an 11-inch plastic worm to be too large for weakfish, but remember, it's tiderunner weaks that will be patrolling the lighthouse rocks, and those big fish possess both the appetite and ability to gulp down large lures and baits. Plus, Dressler said 11-inch worms seem to "float" (sweep with the current) better and move more naturally with the current than smaller worms. Dressler recommends Phenom worms in solid black or black worms with red fire tails.

The plastic worm or Bass Assassin is threaded on a leadhead and cast across the current and toward the boulders. The angler should not begin to reel in, instead, the bait should be allowed to sweep with the current back behind the boat as it sinks toward the bottom. It's important to use a leadhead that is just heavy enough to make the lure sink slowly as it's pushed along by the current. A running current will require a 1-ounce leadhead while a leadhead of one-quarter-ounce is usually adequate during slower water (it is usually necessary to change leadheads several times to adjust to changing tidal conditions). The angler should gently jig the lure as it is slowly sinking and then bouncing along the bottom as it is pushed along with the current. When the lure swings directly behind the boat, it should be jigged up and allowed to fall back to the bottom several times. Then it's time to retrieve and make another cast.

Monofilament line can be used to successfully float worms, yet in this type of fishing there are some definite advantages to super-braided lines such as Berkley Fire Line, Spider Wire, T.U.F. lines and Bass Pro Shops' Nitro line. Their increased sensitivity makes it much easier to detect when a weakfish has inhaled the lure. The line's no-stretch characteristics provide for rapid and easy hooksets. Plus, superbraided lines are thinner in diameter than monofilament of the same strength, and that results in less water resistance and a more natural presentation as worms float and wash in the current. Dressler's favorite outfit for worming the lighthouses is a Daiwa Emblem Z spinning reel, spooled with Berkley Fire Line and mounted on a 6-foot medium-action St. Croix or Shimano rod.

A soft plastic on a leadhead jig is a productive weakfish catcher when cast to rock piles such as lighthouses and jetties. Many bites will come as the current pushes the jig along.

Wind is always a factor in fishing, especially when using this approach to probe lighthouse boulders. It can be unsafe to fish when the wind tends to push an anchored boat toward the lighthouse rocks; when anchoring, be sure the boat is positioned within a long cast of the rocks, but far enough away that it won't be pushed into them by the wind. When fishing into the wind, casting can be cumbersome and the wind will often blow a bow in the line, making it difficult to detect strikes.

The most effective leadhead weight will vary from lighthouse to lighthouse, depending mostly upon the depth of the water, strength of the current, and wind conditions. Different areas along the same lighthouse may be more productive than others during certain stages of the tide and current, and it often pays to move around and experiment until a specific pattern can be determined. It may take a little time to get the hang of this type of fishing, but once a comfort level is developed this approach to fishing lighthouses often pays off in a big way.

While very productive, floating plastics on leadheads is in no way the only effective method for fishing lighthouse rocks. Weakfish are also plucked from the boulders by anglers who cast and retrieve bucktails, leadheads with plastics, spoons and other lures. Lures that are cast directly to the point where the lighthouse rocks meet the water, and that are worked slowly back to the boat just above the submerged rocks, will usually trigger the most strikes. While anglers in both anchored and drifting boats will catch fish, an anchored boat usually provides the most convenient and safest approach to fishing lighthouse boulders.

Weakfish on the rocks will also blast live bait, such as spot, bunker, mullet, eels, small croaker (hardhead) and white perch. Because live baits almost always swim down toward the bottom when hooked and cast, only a light sinker is needed. A common rig for this type of live bait fishing features a sliding egg sinker which is slipped on the line, and then a swivel is tied to the end of the line. Tied to the other end of the swivel is a two to three-feet piece of 30 to 50-pound test mono leader that holds a 5/0 to 7/0 live bait hook. In fact, a heavy sinker will probably only increase snags in the submerged rocks.

Inlets

A lot happens as water moves in and out of inlets. As water from the ocean (incoming tide), or back bays, sounds and tidal rivers (outgoing tide), is funneled through inlets, it carries with it bait, creates differences in water temperatures, forms rips as it tumbles over bottom structure, and swirls around any jetty boulders, piers and bridge pilings that may be present. When these numerous fish-attracting characteristics of inlets are considered, it's easy to understand why big predators patrol them in search of meals.

A moving current during a rising or falling tide will create the best conditions for fish to feed and will enable boating anglers to cover a significant expanse of water. However, it's important to concentrate on specific locations within an inlet that are likely to hold the most fish. They include all areas of water with rips and eddies on the surface; they indicate the presence of bottom structure below and also areas where small baitfish may be overpowered or become disoriented in the strong, swirling current. For weakfish and speckled trout, bait and lures should be lowered to the bottom and bounced along as the boat drifts through the inlet and over the structure. Live baits such as spot, croaker and mullet, and lures including plugs, bucktails and leadheads with plastic twisters, should also be drifted, or cast, as closely as possible to jetty rocks, bridge pilings and other objects in the inlet that water swirls around. Give line and allow them to be pushed along by the current, or retrieve them very slowly. In-line sinkers, or three-way swivel rigs with sinkers of considerable weight, may be required to keep lures and baits near the bottom in a strong current. Pay particular attention to any bends or turns in an inlet, as they often feature swirling water and bottom structure that hold fish.

During times of little or no current in an inlet, when there are no rips and swirls in sight, weakfish and speckled trout can be caught on plugs including Bombers, Rapalas, Rat-L-Traps, MirrOlures and Storm plugs that are cast and slowly retrieved very near jetty boulders and bridge pilings.

Never just drift blindly through an inlet, instead, search out "fishy areas" and thoroughly work those locations by drifting over them, or casting to them, with baits and artificials.

Weakfish and speckled trout are primarily nocturnal feeders, and best bites often come in the evenings, early mornings and overnight. There's much less boat traffic and other disturbances at these times, and weaks and specks will be more aggressive. Be sure to fish any areas of water in an inlet that are illuminated by lights on bridges, piers, docks or nearby buildings. Clouds of baitfish will be drawn to the lights, and predators will hide along the shadow lines and ambush the bait.

In some areas, during the spring and fall, an outgoing tide may be most productive. That's because during high tide, the water in relatively shallow back bay and tidal river areas may have been warmed by the sun. The temperature difference between this back bay water and the water in the inlet and ocean may be only a degree or two,

Inlets are prime weakfish locations. As an incoming or outgoing tide funnels water in or out of the inlet, it carries with it grass shrimp, baitfish and other potential weakfish meals.

but as this warmer water moves through an inlet on a falling tide it may be just warm enough to trigger a good bite from fish that had previously had lockjaw in the cooler water. In the summer, an incoming tide moving cooler water from the ocean and into an inlet may put fish on the feed.

Safety cannot be overemphasized. In some inlets, a hard-running current will at times move water through an inlet with such force and speed that it can be very difficult to fish effectively, or the hard current may create high seas and dangerous boating conditions. Big boats running through an inlet may kick up a large wake that could potentially swamp any inattentive anglers in smaller boats, or push them into nearby jetties or pilings. Anglers drifting an inlet need to be constantly aware of their exact position and surroundings–even while battling big fish–to prevent their boat from colliding with other boats and objects in an inlet.

Weaks And Specks On Wrecks And Reefs

Well known for producing blackfish (tautog), sea bass, cod, pollock, amberjack and spadefish, wrecks and artificial reefs can also be hot spots for big weakfish and speckled trout. Wrecks and reefs support and attract a wide variety of life, including marine plant life, tiny crustaceans, an assortment of small fish and baitfish, right on up to high-order predators.

The first order of business is locating wrecks and reefs. Some charts, including The Fishing Chart Series by Captain Vic Galgano (call 732.821.8810), include a comprehensive listing of wrecks, reefs, snags, lighthouses, shoals, buoys, inlets and other points of interest in the area covered by the particular chart, plus their LORAN TDs and lat/lon coordinates. *The Fisherman* magazine frequently publishes stories containing the exact locations of wrecks and reefs. A number of books available through *The Fisherman* Library (732.295.8600), contain extensive lists of LORAN TDs and lat/lon coordinates. Many coastal states have an artificial reef program that you can contact for information on what materials were used in building their reefs, when they were established, what fish can be found on them, and where the productive structures are located. Become a regular at a tackle shop or two, and as those folks get to know you they may provide valuable information as to the whereabouts of local wrecks. Check various fishing-related sites on the Internet as a number of bait and tackle shop operators, and also fishermen, will share some of their TDs and coordinates over the Internet. Attend as many fishing seminars as possible. To become a successful wreck fisherman, you'll need to do the legwork necessary to develop a comprehensive and accurate listing of wrecks and reefs in the areas you fish, and their exact locations.

Those new to fishing wrecks and artificial reefs will find that the real challenge often comes in anchoring and holding proper position directly on top of the structure. When wreck and reef fishing, lures and baits must be fished directly in the structure, or just over it - fishing a few feet off of a wreck or reef is often fruitless. When the boat arrives at the desired LORAN or lat/lon coordinates, toss over a marker buoy. If the structure isn't seen on the fishfinder, a search must be undertaken. Slowly circle the buoy while keeping one eye peeled on the fishfinder. Start by making small circles around the buoy and gradually expand to bigger and bigger circles until the structure is located, then immediately mark the spot with a second buoy and enter the coordinates into the LORAN or GPS. Slowly motor over the location several times until it becomes clear exactly how the wreck or reef is positioned on the bottom. These subsequent passes may also turn up smaller pieces of wreckage which receive less fishing pressure and are often quite productive.

When the precise location of the wreck or reef has been pinpointed, the next challenge is to strategically drop anchor where the wind and tide will carry the boat back directly over the wreck. One

Concrete culvert is dropped to the bottom as an artificial reef is established. Reefs hold an amazing variety of baitfish and predators, including big weakfish and speckled trout.

approach is to retrieve the original buoy and then return to the marker floating directly above the structure. Then allow the wind and current to move the boat away from the wreck to determine the exact direction of the drift. The next step is to run the boat straight upcurrent and past the marker buoy on top of the wreck. Drop anchor and play out line until the boat drifts back to the buoy marking the wreck site, then tie the anchor line to a bow cleat.

Some savvy wreck fishermen use two buoys tied together to easily determine the direction of the drift and exactly where the boat should be positioned when the anchor is lowered. This set-up features a sinker or sash weight tied to a detergent bottle with a length of heavy fishing line. A second detergent bottle is tethered directly to the first marker buoy with about 25 to 50 feet of fishing line. The first marker buoy is held in place by the sinker or weight on the bottom, and the wind and current push the second bottle away from it - in exactly the same direction the boat will drift once the anchor is lowered. The captain positions the boat upcurrent of the bottles so the boat and the two bottles are in a straight line. Then the anchor is dropped and the boat allowed to drift back to the first bottle which is directly over the wreck.

Anchors fashioned from metal bars used to reinforce concrete (rebar) are used by some anglers to hold the boat right on top of the

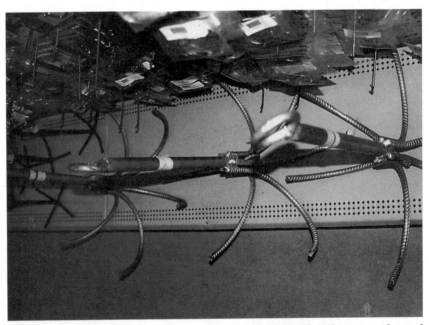

Wreck and reef fishermen looking to position the boat directly over a piece of structure often deploy anchors like these fashioned from metal bars normally used to reinforce concrete.

A fat weakfish caught on a soft plastic bait that was cast and slowly retrieved directly over an artificial reef.

structure. The boat is moved upcurrent of the wreck, the anchor is pitched overboard and the drifting boat drags the anchor along the bottom until the rebar hooks latch onto the structure. Then the anchor rope is shortened as much as possible and tied off on the bow cleat.

Finally, it's time to fish. Weaks and specks on wrecks and reefs can be caught on basic bottom rigs fished straight down in the structure. Bait up with typical trout baits, including squid strips, clam, bloodworms or seaworms, chunks of peeler crab, or cut spot, mullet and bluefish. Snags are often frequent and frustrating, but if you're not getting snagged at least occasionally then you're probably not fishing where the fish are, which is right in the structure. To cut down on lost tackle, many wreck fishermen tie up their own rigs that feature only a surgeon's end loop tied at the bottom to hold the sinker, and a dropper loop tied about a foot above the sinker to hold the hook–no spinners, beads or other hardware are used. Use 50-pound leader material to help fight abrasion as the rig will rub up against sharp edges on wrecks and reefs. Occasionally check the line and leader for nicks and frays by pulling it through your thumb and forefinger, and immediately cut off line or replace leaders that show any damage whatsoever–do not wait until a big fish is hooked and puts on pressure to find out that the line or leader was weakened or damaged!

To reduce the number of snags, some anglers will use in-line sinkers or drail sinkers on their wreck rigs, as these narrow-profile sinkers hang up in structure less often than wider sinkers.

Bucktails, diamond jigs and other metals and spoons jigged just over a wreck will also elicit strikes from weakfish and speckled trout. Drop them down until they hit bottom, make two or three turns on the reel handle, then jig them over the structure by raising and lowering the rod tip. Another approach is to anchor the boat so it comes to rest just off to one side of the wreck or reef. Then cast a bucktail, leadhead with a plastic tail, plug or spoon up ahead of the boat and structure; as the lure slowly sinks the current will push it back to the wreck or reef, as the angler slowly reels it in over the structure.

Live baits such as spot, croaker, porgy, snapper bluefish, mullet and bunker are also very effective when fished on, over and very

A productive method for catching weakfish and speckled trout holding on wrecks and reefs is to simply drop bottom jigs down onto the structure.

near wrecks and reefs. Fairly heavy tackle is recommended when fishing on wrecks and reefs, as that structure is also inhabited by other big predators such as chopper blues and stripers. During one springtime Delaware Bay artificial reef fishing trip with Gene and Kelly Racz from R & R Sports Center in Lewes, Delaware, I hooked and reeled to the surface a weakfish of about 14 inches. Just as I was about to lift it in the boat a huge striper swirled across the surface, grabbed that weakie, took off and instantly broke my 10-pound test line with a loud "crack"! Later, as Kelly Racz was catching weakies on the artificial reef by casting to it with a Halco Trembler, he hooked into something huge. After a 45-minute battle on 10-pound line, Kelly managed to subdue a citation 29-pound striper. It happens every year - so be ready to rumble when you fish wrecks and reefs!

Chapter Seven

MORE "SUPER" STRUCTURE FOR WEAKS AND SPECKS

Small baitfish move onto shoals, sloughs, wrecks, rocks and other changes in the bottom to seek refuge from predators. Mussels, crabs and other critters attach themselves to bridge pilings and jetty boulders to feed upon the marine plant life that grows there. And wherever there are little fish and small crabs, big fish will not be too far away. Structure also provides fish with a current break; fish can get out of the direct current and save energy by positioning themselves downcurrent of structure. Structure also provides predators with ambush points from which they can pounce upon baitfish that get caught up in a hard current and that tumble along as the current collides with and washes around structure.

In fishing, just as it is in real estate, it's location, location, location that makes all the difference! A brand-new tricked-out fishing boat, finest quality tackle and proper techniques will be of little benefit unless used in areas that contain fish. I cannot stress it enough. It does no good to fish where there are no fish. Fish are found on structure, and that goes for all of our favorite species, including everything from weakfish and fluke, to cobia and cod, to tuna and sharks.

The previous chapter was about weakfish and speckled trout structure that are fished by boating anglers. However, surfcasters and other fishermen on foot also have access to a wonderful variety of natural and manmade structure that attract and hold fish. From the beaches to jetties to bridges, the Atlantic Coast features plenty of locations where anglers enjoy easy and inexpensive fishing opportunities with weaks and specks. In fact, both shore-bound fishermen and boating anglers enjoy some of the very best fishing of the entire season at these near-shore and easy-to-reach areas.

Surf Fishing For Weaks And Specks

Locating and fishing structure should be a critical component of any surf fishing strategy. Two of the most abundant and obvious surf structures are sand bars and sloughs. Sand bars most often form just off the beach, and waves will break over them as water moving toward the beach encounters the relatively shallow sand bars. Anglers can identify sand bars by the line of white water (waves) that runs along the sand bar, usually fairly parallel to the beach, and/or by spotting the lighter-colored water that is sometimes evident over the sand bar which is shallower than the surrounding (darker) water. Some sand bars will be far enough off the beach to be out of casting range. When the water and air temperature, wind and tide, and other conditions permit, some dedicated surf fishermen will even wade or swim out to the bar and stand on it to fish beyond the bar, and between the bar and beach.

Surfcasters need to keep an eye out for cuts in sand bars. These especially productive surf fishing spots can be located by looking for areas in the line of white water over the sand bar where the waves don't break and where there is no white water. This opening in the white water indicates an opening (cut) in the sand bar below. The water at the cut is deeper than the water over the shallower sand bar and waves usually will not break over the cut. Baitfish and predators swim through sand bar cuts to gain access to the beach, and again to move off the beach to deeper water beyond the bar. Be sure to cast baits and lures to all sand bar cuts within casting distance.

Sloughs are areas of deeper water that are found between the beach and the sand bar off the beach. They usually feature relatively calm and darker-colored water. Weakfish and other predators will patrol sloughs in search of baitfish and crabs that come tumbling into the slough in the waves that break over the sand bar, and also for sand fleas and other morsels that are swept into the slough by water running back off the beach. It's a vast ocean, and a common temptation for many surf fishermen is to lean back, tense up and heave their bait or lure just as far as they can. Yet, in many cases, these long-distance casts result in the bait or lure flying over

SURF FLOAT RIG

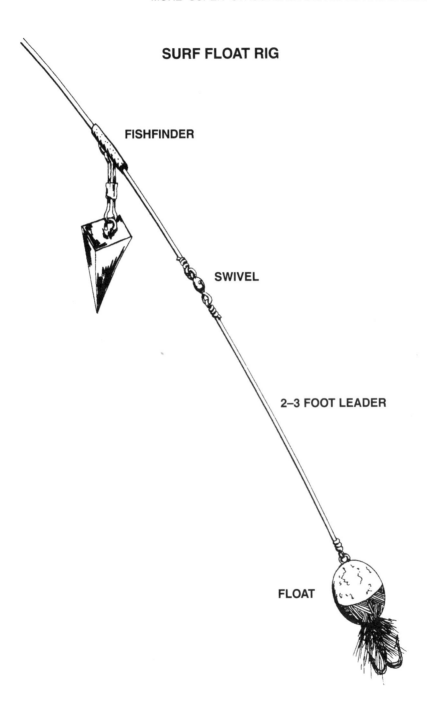

FISHFINDER

SWIVEL

2–3 FOOT LEADER

FLOAT

and way out past the fish. Often, fish are literally right at the feet of surfcasters, gulping down baitfish and crabs in the slough. Be sure to always make at least a couple of casts that travel no more than several feet and splash down just off the beach–the results are often pleasantly surprising!

Some surf fishermen visit their favorite beaches at low tide during the daytime to get a good look at their fishing grounds. They jot down detailed notes and take photos of any noticeable structure or bottom configuration that probably won't be visible during high water and/or at night. Some serious surfcasters even visit the beach with a hand-held GPS so they can punch in the lat/lon of a good-looking spot and then use the GPS later to return to the exact same spot.

The best surf fishing of the entire year draws near in September as summer wanes and fall approaches. The sun drops from sight a little earlier each evening as the days grow noticeably shorter and the nights cooler with each passing week. Less daylight and falling water temperatures prompt many species of fish, including weakfish, to bunch up, chow down and scoot south along the Atlantic Coast, providing anglers with the most exciting surf fishing action of the entire season.

A fantastic bait for fall weakfish is live spot. At times it may be a challenge to obtain, transport and keep spot alive, but whenever and wherever possible, serious surf fishermen will catch their own spot or make arrangements to purchase them through a tackle shop. The extra effort is well worth it because migrating fall weakfish, looking to fatten up for the long winter ahead, simply cannot resist the delicious and nutritious dining opportunities provided by spot.

While conventional and spinning outfits can be used, most of the surf fishing sharpies I know use a conventional reel on a nine to 10-foot surf rod rated for 2-1/2 to 3 ounces, and a reel spooled with 14-pound to 17-pound test monofilament. A fish-finder rig with a 24-inch leader of 30-pound test, and a 5/0 to 7/0 hook, is commonly used. Some anglers are able to cast farther and reach fish holding off the beach with a Long Ranger fish-finder rig from Breakaway Tackle. Spot are commonly hooked through the eyes. Some anglers prefer to use a bass casting sinker with their fish-finder rig because it will roll around in the surf and bring movement to the rig.

There's no doubt that live spot are a prime surf bait, yet hungry weakfish prowling the beaches will also whack other live and cut baits, including mullet, snapper bluefish, squid, eels, sand fleas, bunker and croaker. They can be fished on either fish-finder rigs, bottom rigs with a float near the hook to keep the bait slightly off the bottom and away from bait-stealing crabs (like a surf float rig), and three-way swivel rigs with the sinker tied to one swivel eye while the leader with a 5/0 hook and bait is tied to the other swivel eye.

Many weakfish and speckled trout taken in the surf are caught in the slough, which is an area of relatively deeper and calmer water, usually running parallel to the beach.

When it comes to artificials, bucktails are a "must-have" item. A strip of pork rind, squid or other cut bait, or a plastic tail or twister, is usually attached to the hook to bring additional movement, scent and flavor to the bucktail. Bucktails can be cast out and retrieved slowly and steadily to resemble a swimming baitfish. They can be cast out, allowed to sink to the bottom, then pulled up and off the bottom and toward the beach as the angler makes a long sweep of the rod tip. At the end of the sweep the bucktail sinks to the bottom and the slack is reeled in and the process started again. Anglers can enticingly bounce bucktails along the bottom, and kick up puffs of sand and/or mud similar to a burrowing crab or shrimp, by casting them out, allowing them to sink, and then twitching the rod tip and slowly reeling in the line. When weakfish have their noses to the bottom and are feeding on sand eels, a productive retrieve is reel so slowly that the bucktail is dragged across the bottom. These presentations are also very effective when used with leadhead jigs dressed with plastic tails, and jigs and spoons.

Plugs are also important items in any surf bag or beach buggy. Rebel, Bomber, Yo-Zuri, MirrOlure, Rat-L-Trap, Bagley's, Storm and Creek Chub are but a few of the companies that provide us with excellent plugs that feature realistic finishes and lifelike action that ring the dinner bell for hungry weakfish and other predators. It's important to as closely as possible match the plug size, shape and color to that of the prevalent bait. Floating plugs, and plugs with short lips that dip just below the surface, are the choice when weakfish are feeding near the top of the water. When the bait and weakfish are holding near the bottom, then it's time for sinking plugs and plugs with longer lips that dive deep. Generally, plugs work better on calm days and nights when they're easier to cast and control.

A great way to enhance the effectiveness of a plug or spoon is to rig a teaser ahead it. The following all make tempting teasers: small bucktails, shad darts, flies, and small plastic worms and grubs. During the retrieve, the teaser resembles a small baitfish that is being hotly pursued by a bigger fish (the plug or bucktail behind it).

Teasers can be added to a rig in a number of ways. Some anglers will tie a dropper loop in the leader ahead of the plug or bucktail, and slip the teaser on over the loop. Another method is to tie a barrel swivel to the end of the main line. Two different lengths of leader are then tied to the other eye of the swivel: a two to three-foot piece of leader with the plug or bucktail tied on the other end, and a six to 10-inch leader with the teaser tied on. The dropper loop or leader used to hold the teaser should be short to prevent the teaser from wrapping around and tangling with the leader holding the plug or spoon.

Speck rigs, which are two bucktails or shad darts tied in tandem so that one trails slightly behind the other (just like a teaser ahead of

To increase success in the surf, astute fishermen visit the beach at low tide during daylight hours to observe bars and drop-offs that are otherwise covered during times of high tide.

a plug or bucktail), are very popular among surf fishermen who target speckled trout, especially in the Outer Banks of North Carolina. Speck rigs can be purchased in many tackle shops, or anglers can easily and quickly tie their own using a dropper loop, or two leaders from a barrel swivel as described in the previous paragraph.

Shallows

In many areas, spring features perhaps the most exciting, easily-accessible weakfish action of the entire year. Anglers enjoy shallow-water, light-tackle, small boat fishing thrills at near-shore locations such as canals, inlets, tidal creeks and along the beachfront. The water in the ocean and bays is still cool in late April and May, often below the 52 to 55-degree range that will usually trigger a consistent weakfish bite. However, shallow water in canals, creeks and along the beach can be warmed rather quickly by the sun, especially on clear, bright days. Shallow water will often be a few degrees warmer than nearby deeper water, and those few degrees can make all the difference in the world when it comes to catching weakfish. Warm, shallow water provides weakfish with more than just comfort. These locations are also prime feeding areas, as baitfish will seek out the warmest water they can find in the spring.

Many inlets may not be particularly shallow, but the water in them will be relatively warm on a falling tide. During incoming and high tide, cool water from the ocean will move through an inlet and into shallow canals and back bays where it is warmed by the sun. Then, as the tide starts to fall, that warmed water is funneled back through the inlet where it often prompts a feeding spree by weakfish and other predators.

Weakfish are plenty hungry in the spring after passing a long, cold winter offshore. Shallow, warm water that's often loaded with baitfish and crabs provides them with perfect opportunities to satiate their voracious appetites. It also enables fishermen to shake off their winter doldrums in grand style. And perhaps best of all, these spring hot spots are easy for anglers to get at. Fishermen on foot, and small-boat anglers, visit piers, jetties, beaches, bridges and other highly-accessible locations for fantastic, springtime weakfish action.

A top weakfish bait in the spring is a chunk of shedder or peeler crab. A small chunk of shedder crab, fished on bottom rigs or buck-tails (run the hook through a socket where a leg has been removed), provides the offering with scent and flavor that trigger strikes from early-season weaks and specks. Shedder crabs can be all but impossible to buy at tackle shops in April and early May, and many anglers in recent seasons have found a very productive substitute in chicken. Packaged chicken breast is purchased at grocery stores - even some tackle shops now carry it - and cut into strips that are used to provide tantalizing scent and flavor to bottom rigs.

While the emergence of chicken as a good bait has been a hot topic of discussion in recent seasons, springtime shallow-water weakfish will also whack other baits and lures. Some tackle shops sell frozen peelers which have been stored in freezers since the previous season. Live, fresh shedder crabs are always better than frozen shedders, yet frozen crabs can be used to catch fish when live crabs aren't available. Squid strips and bloodworms will also put weakfish in the cooler. These baits are fished on Maw's Tails, Delaware Bay Green Machines and other Captain Mitchell rigs, Pop's Rigs, fish-finder rigs, and any number of store-bought and homemade bottom rigs.

Artificial lures that will provoke weakfish strikes include MirrOlures, Rat-L-Traps, Yo-Zuri plugs, Halco Tremblers, Bomber plugs, Rapala plugs, Gotcha plugs, shad darts, speck rigs, and also leadhead jigs dressed with plastic tails, including Fin-S Fish and Berkley Power Worms. The key when targeting springtime weakfish with these lures is to work them low and slow in the weakfish strike zone on or very near the bottom.

Bridges

Bridges cast shadows, interrupt the current, grow food, create hiding places and, best of all, attract weakfish and speckled trout. Many of the largest weaks and specks taken each and every season are hooked by anglers who recognize and take advantage of the outstanding fishing opportunities provided by bridges.

Bridge pilings, abutments or supports create a chain of life that begins with algae, mussels, shrimp and crabs that grow on and hang on these structures. Baitfish (including minnows, eels, small white perch, bergalls, tiny bluefish and others) move in and pick those tasty morsels off the pilings. Then much bigger fish, including weaks and specks, visit the pilings to eat the baitfish.

As the current collides with pilings, abutments or supports, the water rushes and tumbles around the structure, creating a spot of relatively calm water just behind or directly downcurrent of the piling or support. Fish get out of the current, hold tight to the piling and rest in this calm water. These spots are also great ambush points. Weaks and specks in the calm pockets will dart out from behind the piling to grab smaller fish and crabs as they are swept past in the current.

Bridges provide fantastic fishing opportunities for both boat anglers and fishermen on foot. The calm-water pockets just behind pilings are favorite ambush points of predators like weakfish.

BRIDGE SHADOW LINE

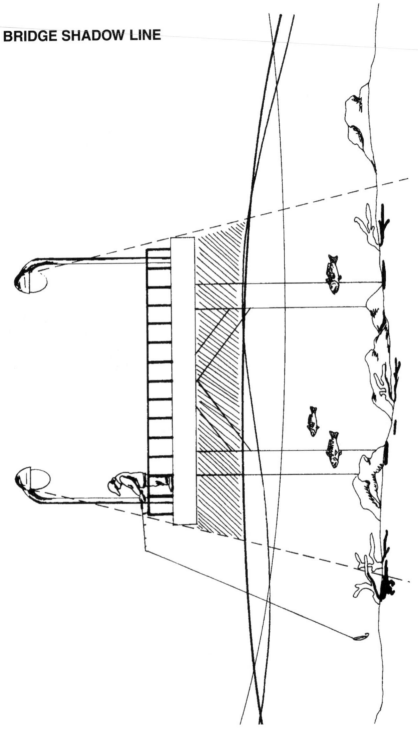

The current washing around bridge structure can also scour the bottom and create nearby holes and pockets that attract and hold fish.

Often, there is even more fish-attracting structure at the base of bridge pilings and supports. Boulders or concrete are sometimes used to reinforce supports where they enter the bottom of the bay, ocean or river. While the bridge was being built, a considerable amount of construction material probably fell (or was tossed) from the bridge into the water and sank. Over the years, debris floating with the current will strike the bridge pilings and sink alongside of them. Although it's illegal, some people toss their junk off bridges. Some of this material breaks up and washes away, yet a lot of it piles up and accumulates near the bridge, much like an artificial reef.

Bridges give up big fish both day and night, yet there's something almost surreal about fishing bridges after dark. Shadows and shadow lines, especially under and around lighted bridges, are perhaps a bridge's most exciting "structure". At night, baitfish will swarm under bridge lights shining on the water in much the same manner that moth and bugs fly around a street light. The ability to see bunches of tightly-packed baitfish holding just under the surface in areas illuminated by bridge lights, and then to witness weaks and specks crashing through them, provide an incredible angler adrenaline rush. Weakfish and speckled trout become considerably more aggressive and feed much closer to the surface at night. Plus it's usually quieter at night, with significantly less boat traffic than during the daytime.

On some bridges it's possible and legal to fish from the bridge itself, which provides easy and exciting access to big fish below. For example, some of the biggest and most impressive weakfish taken in Ocean City, Maryland, each season, are hooked by anglers fishing lures and baits from the Route 50 bridge.

Boating anglers can use a number of tactics to effectively fish bridges for big weaks and specks. When current and wind conditions allow, it is possible to cast lures and live bait to bridge supports and shadow lines as the boat drifts under the bridge. Yet actual fishing time–time spent near or under the bridge and within casting range of the structure–will be relatively brief. Drifting demands a lot of repositioning the boat for new drifts. Plus, high angler attentiveness is required when drifting bridges, especially at night. It's easy to lose track of what's going on around you, especially when a fish is hooked or a lure is snagged. It only takes a brief moment or two of lost concentration for the boat to drift into the bridge, or for some other potentially troublesome development to occur. At least two anglers–two sets of eyes and ears–should probably be on board when drifting bridges.

Bridges can be effectively and safely fished from an anchored boat. A common approach is to drop anchor well upcurrent of the bridge, allow the boat to drift back to within casting range of the structure or shadow line, and then tie off the anchor line. Anglers in the back of the boat can then work the pilings by casting to them with a bucktail or a leadhead dressed with a plastic twister tail, or a swimming plug. Another effective tactic involves the use of a baitcasting reel or small conventional reel. A small artificial lure or a lightly-weighed bottom rig with live or cut bait is dropped off the back of the boat and to the bottom. The angler uses his thumb to control the spool and play out line as the current pushes the offering along the bottom and back toward the bridge where waiting fish will grab it.

Weaks and specks usually hold deep during the daytime, and trollers get down to them by pulling bucktails, plugs and spoons with wire line, superbraided lines and heavy sinkers. The sinker and rig are bounced along the bottom as the boat is slowly motored parallel to the bridge pilings. Trolling is usually done on the upcurrent side of the bridge, so the current will push the rig toward the structure and the fish. The angler working the rod raises and lowers the rod tip to ensure that the sinker is bouncing on the bottom (additional line is let out when contact with the bottom is not detected). The angler also needs to keep the sinker bouncing in order to prevent it from constantly lodging in the rocks and debris commonly found on the bottom near bridges. Snags can be frequent and frustrating, but remember, the same stuff that snags bottom rigs also attracts fish.

Bridges provide fish with an abundance of food and shelter, and anglers targeting trophy weaks and specks should not fail to take full advantage of these wonderful fishing opportunities.

Jetties

Fishermen on foot, and anglers in boats, both have access to the many different predatory fish that come to jetties to feed. Visit a jetty at low tide in the daytime and you'll see algae and other marine plant life, plus mussels and barnacles, clinging to the rocks. When the tide comes up and submerges those plants and crustaceans, then minnows, mullet, eels, crabs, lobster, spot, croaker, white perch and tautog move in to feed among the boulders. Then bigger predators, including weaks, specks, striped bass, bluefish and fluke, show up and chow down on the minnows, mullet, spot, croaker and other small fish.

Casting distance is not a priority on jetties, in fact, casting far and away from the rocks is counter productive, as it puts the lure out of the strike zone. Weaks, specks and other predators poke around right in among the rocks for their food, so casts and retrieves should

JETTY STRUCTURE

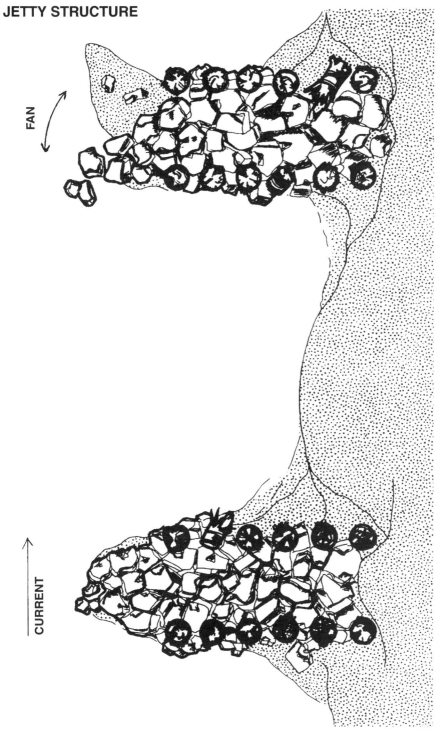

FAN

CURRENT

165

be made that keep the bait or lure near the rocks for as long as possible. Anglers standing on a jetty should cast off to one side, and then to the other side, so the retrieves bring the lure back practically parallel to the rocks, and close to the rocks. A lot of fish will be hooked right at the angler's feet, often just before the lure is lifted out of the water for the next cast. Boating anglers need to make sure their casts splashdown right where the jetty boulders meet the water.

Jetties are excellent locations for livelining with baitcasting and conventional tackle. That's because weaks and specks snoop around jetty rocks specifically for spot, croaker, mullet and snapper bluefish. A rig featuring very little or no weight is typically used. Both anglers in boats and on the jetty should lob the live bait near the rocks and allow it to wash with the current. A drop-back is required when a pickup is detected. Then all of the slack is reeled in and the hook is set with authority. Bucktails and leadheads dressed with plastic tails, and swimming plugs, all catch weaks and specks on jetty rocks because they closely resemble the baitfish naturally attracted to the boulders.

With live baits and lures, leaders as heavy as 50-pound test are used to fight the abrasion that the leader endures when a big hooked weakfish or speckled trout rubs the leader against barnacle-encrusted jetty rocks.

Extreme caution must be a priority among both boating anglers and those fishermen who walk out onto jetties. It's important to remember that there's a lot more to jetties than what meets the eye. Jetties are pounded by high winds and rough seas, and they will fall apart, meaning some rocks have tumbled away and are nearby, either submerged or partially-submerged. While these stray boulders are great fish attractors, boaters must take care to avoid bringing their motor and boat into contact with them. Sea conditions must be constantly monitored so that a sudden and surprisingly large wave doesn't push the boat onto the rocks. Large waves breaking over a jetty are also a threat to anglers standing on the rocks.

A running current almost always features more productive fishing than times of little or no water movement. During the heat of the summer, the night shift is far and away the best time to hit the jetties. Moving water at sunset, and at first light, can also be times of great action. Daytime action with weakfish and speckled trout on jetties improves in September, October and November. Overcast days can be especially rewarding.

To venture out onto the slippery rocks of a jetty without a pair of Korkers or at least golf cleats is to invite a painful and perhaps dangerous spill. Jetty jocks also need to dress properly to stay dry and warm in the sometimes inhospitable elements (breaking waves, wind) often encountered on a jetty. Rain gear is a must. Tops and bottoms must be worn for comfort and safety. It's often a good idea to wear knee-high boots under rain gear pants to keep your feet and legs high and dry (don't forget the Korkers which go on over top of the boots). Warmth and mobility are needed on jetties, so wear several layers of light clothing; avoid thick and bulky clothing that makes it tough to get around on the rocks. Keep a complete change of dry clothing in the truck or car in case of an accidental soaking. Since a lot of successful jetty fishing is done in the dark, wear a flashlight around your neck on a lanyard for easy access. A flashlight is vital for carefully navigating wet and slippery rocks, and for changing lures and unhooking fish in the dark. A vest is a jetty jock's tackle box, and should feature pockets and compartments bulging with plugs, bucktails, plastic worms, leadheads, spoons and other lures of all sizes, shapes and colors. Many anglers will hang a shower curtain clip from a loop on their vest. The clip is used to keep handy in-line sinkers which are often needed to get a bucktail or leadhead down deep, especially during times of moving water. Other items which can be clipped on include nail clippers or a small pair of scissors, pliers and a rag. During the daytime, a hat or visor will help keep the sun out of your eyes, and is especially valuable when the sun is low in the sky, such as sunrise and dusk (good weakfish and speckled trout times!) A hat or visor also helps protect sunglasses from splashing water.

Chapter Eight

ELECTRONICS, DRIFTING, ANCHORING, TROLLING AND PARTY BOATS

For many anglers, drifting is the most enjoyable and relaxed way to fish, yet successful drifting requires careful planning and attention to detail. Trolling enables anglers to thoroughly fish large areas and to pinpoint pods of fish when they're spread out. Anchoring requires more physical work than the others, yet it provides the most action when fish are concentrated in small groups. Each approach has its definite advantages, depending upon many factors, including the numbers and distribution of the fish, the structure to be fished, and weather and sea conditions. This chapter looks at when, where and why drifting, anchoring and trolling will offer the best chance at success with weakfish and speckled trout.

There's a lot of water out there, and to catch fish consistently, it's crucial that boating anglers have the ability to locate fish and to get right on top of fish-attracting structure. Weakfish and speckled trout are caught in many of the same spots year after year. Yet each season anglers also discover a few new hot spots. Being aware of these locations is one thing, finding them is quite another. A good eye for shore ranges and land points, and especially marine electronics including LORAN, GPS and DGPS, enable boating anglers to accurately travel back and forth from the ramp to hot spots. Fishfinders enable us to visualize the bottom and the presence of baitfish and predators, including weaks and specks. Electronics make us more efficient and effective fishermen.

This chapter also contains information on several other important items that can be used to increase the effectiveness of your drifting, anchoring and trolling efforts. They include buoys that visually mark a specific productive spot, easy-to-make sea anchor imitations that can put the brakes on a speeding boat and put fish in the cooler, electric motors that enable anglers to troll quietly and sneak up on unsuspecting fish, and wreck anchors that hold a boat directly on top of fish-filled snags and reefs.

Party boats are a great way to get in on weakfish action. These big boats offer stable fishing platforms, and the captains are often aware of some "secret" hot spots that receive little fishing pressure and contain big numbers of fish. The single most exciting weakfish trip of my entire life came aboard a party boat, and it featured hour after hour of furious topwater action with eight-pound weakfish continually flying over the rail!

Electronics

The 20th century has been called an age of science and technology, and to the benefit of anglers everywhere, many inventions and developments have been successfully applied to fishing and boating. Scientists, chemists and researchers have given us amazingly innovative, lightweight, strong, durable, sensitive and long-lasting materials that have been used in the manufacturing of rods, reels, lines, lures and boats. For example, unimaginable to anglers just a few short decades ago, are our modern-day fishing lures that are now loaded with high-tech chemicals that provide lifelike scent and flavor. And in this new millennium we can look forward to continued progress and newer, more exciting technology that will make our pursuit of saltwater and freshwater fish even more enjoyable and successful.

Many would say that fishermen have received the greatest benefit from the developments, improvements and marine applications made in electronics, including fishfinders, LORAN, GPS and DGPS. While it is easy to take them for granted now, trust this forty-something angler when I say that it wasn't too long ago that they weren't readily available, or were very expensive. Now they're commonplace and affordable, yet their importance cannot be overemphasized.

Modern marine electronics enable fishermen to pinpoint and record the exact location of a piece of fish-holding structure and return to that same spot again and again.

Once a piece of fish-holding structure has been located, fishermen may deploy a marker buoy to make it even easier to return to that spot during the day's fishing.

They enable us to pinpoint and record the exact location of fish, bait and fish-attracting structure. They make it possible to return to these hot spots again and again. They enable us to visualize structure and bottom contour, and how baitfish and predators (including weakfish and speckled trout) position themselves on it. In short, marine electronics are our "underwater eyes", and provide us with reliable navigation that make it possible to easily find specific fishing hot spots, and return again safely to port.

While fishfinders and color scopes will indicate the presence of fish below the boat, many anglers say they serve an even greater role. They make it possible to "see" the bottom and identify fish-attracting structure. Fishfinders enable anglers to position their boats directly over shoals, sloughs, wrecks and reefs so that they can concentrate their efforts on the exact spots that hold the greatest number of fish.

While fishfinders and color scopes illustrate the bottom, structure, bait and fish, it's LORAN, GPS and DGPS that enable anglers to travel directly to the areas with productive structure, and to return to them again and again. LORAN uses radio signals and time differential or TD numbers, while GPS and DGPS use signals from satellites in space orbiting the earth and lat/lon coordinates, to provide the location of the boat at that particular moment, and the boat's position in relation to the desired destination. These units will provide (even illustrate) the exact compass heading to travel to reach a desired location, the distance from the current location to the second spot, and in some instances the speed of the boat and the estimated time of arrival. Accuracy to within 50 feet can be expected from LORAN, GPS and DGPS. The TD numbers and lat/lon coordinates for various spots are recorded in the unit and can be called up at will by the operator. The enormous benefits of this technology are obvious and they play a huge role in the consistent success of weakfish and speckled trout anglers who use these valuable tools to find and fish productive structure.

Anglers can use several sources to stockpile lists of TDs and lat/lon numbers for productive fishing areas and ports. Many charts available in tackle shops and marinas feature TDs, and lat/long numbers, for shoals, lighthouses, buoys and inlets. Stories published in *The Fisherman* magazine often contain the numbers for excellent spots. And many of the boat and sportfishing shows held in the fall and winter from New England to Florida will feature seminar speakers who are sometimes willing to share some of their productive locations.

A temperature gauge provides the temperature of the surface water at the location of the boat. Depending on tidal and wind conditions, water temperatures may vary by several degrees from one location to another only a relatively short distance away. This change, which could mean the difference between a nice catch or empty cooler, would be undetected by anglers without a temperature gauge. Early in the season, when the water is still cool, it is a wise choice to fish the warmest water that can be found (if at all possible, search out water that is at least 52 degrees, and preferably 55 degrees). In the summer, when water temperatures in some areas may be 75 to 85 degrees and too warm for weakfish comfort, the recommendation is to fish the coolest water that can be located. Late in the fall, as water temperatures drop, expect the best bites to occur in areas with the warmest water.

Marker Buoys

Marker buoys are valuable aids when it comes to anchoring over wrecks inhabited by weakfish and speckled trout, or to mark a shoal, slough, hole, edge or other specific hot spot where fish have been caught while drifting or trolling. Empty detergent bottles (with the lids on) make good buoys. Use orange and yellow bottles which will be easy to spot on the water. Avoid white, green and blue which are difficult to see.

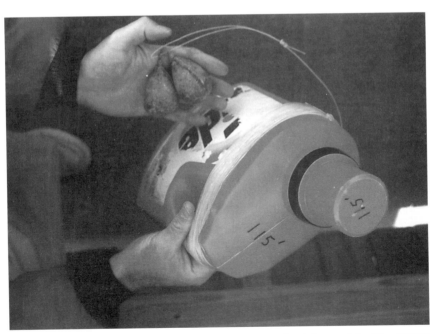

A handy marker buoy can be made from an empty detergent bottle. Bright orange or yellow are good colors.

Tie one end of heavy fishing line such as 100 or 200-pound test mono to the bottle's handle. Heavy sinkers or a sash weight are attached to the other end of the line.

Wrap the line around the bottle so that when tossed overboard, the sinking weight will pull line from the bottle. The bottle will spin on the surface as the line peels off.

Make several buoys with different line lengths for use in different water depths. Use a permanent marker pen to write the line length on the bottle.

Log Book

After a day or night on the water, and after cleaning fish, washing the boat, rinsing tackle and gear, and putting everything in its proper place, many anglers (including yours truly) are ready for a shower, cold drink, hot food and some relaxation. However, there is one last but important task that should be completed while the fishing activities are still fresh in your mind. Enter important information from the trip in a log book. Every fishing trip, from wildly successful to rather slow, should be documented in a log book. It's a good idea to jot down notes on a note pad while on the water, or at least make clear mental notes you'll be able to recall later. Following the fishing trip and clean-up, all information should be condensed and written in the log book. Make sure each entry includes the date, moon phase for that particular day, each location that was fished (TDs for LORAN and lat/lon for GPS), the structure and water depth at each location, and the time of day, tidal and current conditions, wind direction and weather conditions, air and water temperature, and other pertinent information from each fishing location. Note who your fishing partners were that day, how many fish were caught, and also the most productive lures, baits, rigs and techniques.

Some of my friends accuse me of being a cave man who is totally missing out on this age of technology, yet much to their dismay and/or amusement, I continue to maintain my log book the old fashioned way–by writing the information in a notebook. The anglers who accuse me of being behind the times scoff at paper and pencil and instead keep their log book in a computer. I even know of one angler who maintains his fishing notes on tape by speaking them into a hand-held tape recorder. It doesn't matter how it's done, the important point is to make sure that you have a log and keep it up to date. Develop a log book system that's comfortable for you, and stick with it. The older I get the more quickly I forget things. Fishing information that isn't documented in one form or another will be gone in no time, and I'll suffer for it. But writing it down, entering it in a computer or recording it will keep it available and enables anglers to refer to it any-time they want. The more fishing trips that are entered into the log book, the more valuable it becomes. Reviewing the information will make it possible to identify previous hot spots and productive tech-niques that can go a long way toward increasing the success of future fishing trips. Log books are a valuable fishing tool.

Drifting

Drifting involves the boat being moved by the wind and/or cur-rent, which in turn moves the bait or lure through the water. Perhaps the most significant advantage of drifting is that when conditions are favorable, lots of water can be covered, increasing the likeli-hood that fish will be encountered and caught. Since the motor isn't needed to move the boat, drifting is also a quiet way to fish. A stealth approach is especially important when fishing on shallow shoals and lumps, and in skinny water in back bays and tidal rivers, where boat and motor noise can very easily spook fish into deeper water and put them off the feed.

A boat can be stopped and anglers can drift-fish anytime a pod of fish or fishy-looking structure shows up on the fishfinder. However,

When drifting anglers come across a school of weakfish, they should consider dropping anchor so they can concentrate their efforts on that exact spot instead of continuing the drift, which may carry them into unproductive water.

most anglers usually develop a fishing strategy prior to each trip, and they usually have in mind particular structure or locations that they want to fish. A compass, and LORAN or GPS, are used to run directly to the spots. After arriving at the location to be fished, study the wind and current to determine the exact direction the boat will drift. Take great care to precisely position the boat so it will drift directly over the structure and fish. At the starting point of the drift, either drop over a marker buoy, enter the LORAN TDs or lat/lon, or visually check out any shore ranges or land points that may be visible. If the first drift is productive, this makes it possible to return to the exact starting point to begin the second drift. Or, if the first drift didn't turn up fish, then new bottom can be fished on the second drift by beginning the drift to the left or right of the original starting point.

After completing a drift, as the boat is motored into position to begin the next drift, be sure to run well around the area to be fished. Weakfish and speckled trout are easily spooked by boat and motor noise, particularly noise from outboard motors as they run directly over fish on structure in relatively shallow water of 10 to 25 feet deep.

If the bite suddenly comes on strong during a drift, mark the exact spot with another marker buoy, LORAN TDs, lat/lon or land points. Continue drifting, and also mark the spot where the bite seems to slow. Then concentrate the following drifts on that exact area between the buoys where the fish seemed to be congregated. If it's a relatively small area, the best way to fish it may be to anchor up. Before leaving the location, make sure LORAN TDs and other pertinent information are obtained so the exact hot spot can be easily found on future trips.

A number of fishing methods can be employed successfully from a drifting boat. High low rigs and other bait rigs, plus Stingsilvers, Hopkins spoons, Crippled Herrings, Gotcha plugs, bucktails and other jigs will bring strikes as they're bounced along the bottom while the drifting boat carries them over shoals, sloughs, channels and edges. The depth of the water, strength of the current and wind, and type and diameter of the fishing line, will determine how heavy the sinker needs to be to get a bait rig to the bottom. It will be necessary to occasionally let out additional line to keep the rig on the bottom; when the rig gets to be a considerable distance from the boat, reel up and start over. Jigs need to be heavy enough to cut through the current and reach bottom. While raising and lowering the rod tip to jig the lure, the angler should be able to detect the "thump" of the jig hitting bottom when the rod tip is lowered. When contact with bottom is lost, either play out more line or reel up and begin again. In a strong current and/or deeper water, additional time in the strike zone (on the bottom) can be obtained by casting the jig ahead of the drifting boat. This gives the jig time to reach bottom,

ZIG-ZAG DRIFT PATTERN

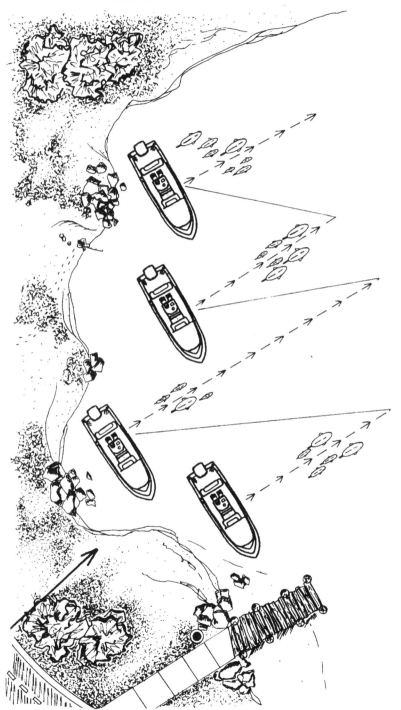

and the angler time to raise and lower the rod tip several times, while the boat drifts toward the jig. It will be necessary to reel in slack as the boat gets closer to the jig. As the boat passes the jig, several more bounces can be made before contact with the bottom is lost and the jig needs to be retrieved.

Weakfish and speckled trout can also be caught by anglers casting plugs, bucktails and other artificials from a drifting boat. This is especially true if the drift carries the boat nearly parallel to a jetty, lighthouse rock pile, bridge or other structure.

Fight The Elements

Unfortunately, most of us do not get to fish nearly as much as we would like. Our jobs, little league baseball games, household and lawn chores, foul weather and other matters seem to conspire to eat up a great deal of our time. That means our time on the water is precious, and we have to make the most of it. One way to do that is to not give up, and to get creative, when the elements work against us.

When drifting and bottom bouncing with bait or jigs, most weakfish and speckled trout will be caught while the current is running and the boat is drifting over productive structure. During incoming or outgoing water, baitfish, crabs and other tasty morsels are swept along by the current and preyed upon by opportunistic weaks and specks. Conversely, everything often comes to a standstill when the current stops, especially when there is little wind to push the boat along. Another time the bite may be slow is when the wind is blowing against the tide and the boat just won't drift. But instead of sitting there wasting away valuable fishing time, do something that may improve the odds.

Savvy anglers will create their own "drift" by moving the boat as slowly as the motor will permit. In addition to the regular motor, some anglers equip their boats with an additional small outboard motor ("kicker motor") specifically for this purpose (it also provides insurance in case of problems with the big motor). Without a kicker motor, a tactic that can be used is to bump the boat's motor in and out of gear just enough to keep the boat moving as if it were drifting.

Largemouth bass anglers commonly cast away while they use their foot to steer and control an electric trolling motor that quietly moves them from blowdown to blowdown, grass-bed to grass-bed. An electric motor can also be a valuable asset for weakfish and speckled trout fishermen, especially anglers who fish back bays and tidal rivers in small fiberglass boats or aluminum boats. They can be used to provide movement to the boat and bait at times of no current, no wind and no natural drift. They can also quietly put the boat in position, and hold it there, while the angler casts artificials to bridge, pier and dock pilings, bulkheads, jetties and other structure.

On the other hand, there will be those days when the boat drifts too fast for productive fishing, especially when a brisk wind is blowing with the current, and/or during periods of a full moon or new moon. During a speedy drift it can be all but impossible to hold bottom or provide a natural presentation of bait and lures. Now the idea is to slow the boat. Sea anchors are sold for this purpose, or anglers can create their own version of a modified sea anchor by tying a length of rope to the handle of a bucket, tossing the bucket overboard, and tying off the other end of the rope to a cleat. The bucket will fill with water and will be dragged through the water and slow the boat.

Anchoring

Anchoring often involves more sweat and hard work than either drifting or trolling, yet there are times when the rewards of anchor-

When the boat is drifting too fast, in a strong current and/or during windy conditions, dragging a bucket to slow the drift can help you catch some big weakfish.

ing make the extra effort worthwhile. One situation to consider dropping anchor is when tightly-packed schools of fish are indicated on the fishfinder. Drifting isn't most effective in this scenario because too much time is spent with the baits outside and away from the fish congregations. As the boat moves over a pile of fish indicated on the fishfinder, mark the spot with a marker buoy or exact LORAN TDs or lat/lon. Then, according to the wind and current, position the boat so that when the anchor is dropped and line is played out and then tied off to a cleat, the boat will come to rest very near the marker buoy or right at the TDs or lat/lon.

A straight up-and-down presentation of baits or lures is usually effective. A typical high/low rig baited with squid or chicken strips, chunks of peeler crab, bloodworms, or cut spot or mullet, dropped to the bottom in the middle of the school, should trigger strikes. Another great way to work over tightly-bunched fish is to vertical jig them with bucktails, leadheads with plastics, and spoons and jigs. Drop them straight to the bottom and jig them up and down by raising and lowering the rod tip a foot or two. Weakfish and speckled trout will jump all over those tempting jigs.

Anchoring is also used to hold the boat in position so anglers can cast to a specific target, usually a bridge piling, dock, lighthouse rock pile or grass-bed. The boat is positioned upcurrent and/or upwind of the structure so that when the anchor is dropped and line

Many bay fishermen use a bridle system to anchor so the boat is sideways to the fish allowing each angler plenty of casting room.

ANCHORING OVER STRUCTURE

played out and tied off, the boat will be within casting distance of the structure. Then anglers can thoroughly fish the structure with bucktails, leadheads, plugs and other lures.

Weakfish and speckled trout anglers also fish at anchor while chumming, and while probing wrecks and reefs for big fish.

Chumming

Chumming involves putting scent and flavor in the water that grab fish by the nose, put them in a feeding mode, and pull them to your baits or lures. It's no different than if you or I would go all day without eating, and then, when we're good and hungry, we walk past a restaurant. The heavenly aroma of delicious meals drifts out, our mouths water, our stomachs grumble, and in we go for something to eat. It's pretty much the same scenario for predatory fish in a chum slick. On those occasions when sea conditions and other factors are perfect, the tantalizing scent and flavor disbursed through the water by chumming will be so enticing that fish will actually swim up to and nudge the chum bucket or boat - all in plain sight of the excited anglers on board.

Weakfish and speckled trout chumming is done from an anchored boat. It's important to anchor and fish near structure, be it a shoal, slough, drop-off, rock pile, wreck or reef. The boat should be anchored upcurrent of the structure, so the chum will drift back to the fish holding on the structure. When they get a whiff and taste of the chum, their appetites and curiosity will be aroused and the fish will follow the chum line in search of a meal. As they move up the chum slick they'll encounter the big juicy baits you have prepared for them, or the artificial lures you are serving them. They'll open wide to chow down and you'll be in business!

Chum can be disbursed through in the water in a number of ways. Frozen chum in a five-gallon bucket with holes drilled in it can be purchased at many bait and tackle shops. A line is tied to the bucket handle and then tied off to a stern cleat and the bucket is dropped over the transom. As the chum inside the bucket melts, bits and pieces of it will wash out through the holes and will be carried away with the current, creating a fish-attracting chum slick. Blocks of frozen chum can also be hung over the side in an onion bag or some other type of mesh bag or netting that's tied off to a stern cleat.

Most of the frozen chum that is purchased in bait and tackle shops is chum made from ground up bunker, also known as menhaden, pogy, fatback and alewive. Mackerel chum is also available in some places at certain times.

Chumming is an effective way to draw weakfish to the boat and keep them there. This angler is chumming for weakfish with grass shrimp.

Some anglers make their own fresh chum by buying or catching live crabs (shedder crabs, speckled crabs, green crabs), and fish (bunker, bluefish, spot, pigfish, croaker) which are then broken up or cut into chunks and pieces. The juicy morsels and entrails are then put in an onion bag that is hung over the side.

Many anglers, especially on Chesapeake Bay, carry meat grinders on their boats. The grinder is often mounted on the gunnel and some sort of fresh or frozen fish, preferably fresh bunker, is inserted. The bloody mess that comes out the other end either drops directly into the water or is ladled overboard.

Chunking, a variation of chumming that involves tossing out by hand cut fish and crabs, will also attract weakfish and speckled trout. Bunker, mullet and other baitfish and crabs are cut into small chunks, about the size of a nickel. A handful of these pieces are occasionally tossed overboard. They'll slowly sink as they're pushed away from the boat by the current. A handful of baits should only be tossed in when the previous baits have sunk and/or drifted out of sight. Remember, you're trying to tempt the fish, not feed them, so don't overdo it. This is practically identical to bunker chunking for striped bass, or chunking for tuna, except on a smaller scale. Live grass shrimp can also be tossed over to attract fish in this manner.

Squid, mussels and clams also make good weakfish and speckled trout chum. Some anglers will mix rice in with their chum for enhanced visual appeal in the slick. Captain Jack Rodgers from Prime Hook Beach in Delaware even chums with cat food in a coffee can while fishing for early-season shallow-water weakfish in Delaware Bay.

Chumming and chunking can get all kinds of gooey fish and crab parts all over the boat, but anglers tolerate it because chumming and chunking also put fish in the cooler. However, in recent years there has been an alternative to the rather sloppy traditional chumming methods, as Glory Hole Fishing Products has marketed a dry chum concentrate that doesn't make a mess. The Glory Hole dry chum concentrate also requires no refrigeration, and what isn't used one day can easily be saved for a future fishing trip. The dry chum concentrate comes in one-pound containers for about three hours of chumming, and eight-pound pails for up to 24 hours of chumming. The concentrate is available in seven flavors, including all-purpose and shrimp which are especially appealing to weakfish and speckled trout. The Glory Hole lineup of fish-attracting products and accessories includes fish oil, and also pots, buckets and other chum-dispensing devices.

No matter which chumming method is used, the key is to keep a steady, uninterrupted flow of chum moving with the current. The chum line should consist of blood and fluids from the fish or crabs,

Chumming will attract plenty of weakfish within casting range for light-tackle fun and lots of action.

and also scales and pieces of shell, and very small morsels of fish and crab flesh. The pieces should be only big enough to stir the appetites of weakfish and speckled trout, and make them crave more, which will prompt them to move up the chum line and encounter your baits. If the pieces are too big, the fish will lay back, away from the boat and baits, and satisfy themselves on the chum. And make sure the flow of chum remains steady. If hungry fish following a chum slick encounter a break in the scent and flavor, they'll probably turn around and head back to where they came from, never to get near the baits.

Weakfish and speckled trout, especially bigger fish, are usually less aggressive during the day. When chumming, many daytime anglers will bottom fish with bait, including shedder crab chunks, bloodworms and seaworms, squid strips, grass shrimp, and fresh cut bluefish or spot. They'll stand in the back of the boat and cast cut bait on a fish-finder rig or some other type of bottom rig into the chum slick behind the boat. The rod can either be held by the angler, or placed in the rod holder with the clicker on.

At night, or early in the mornings, late in the evenings, or on overcast days, when big weaks and specks are more likely to follow a chum line closer to the boat, baits can be "floated" back with the chum. This involves nothing more than tying a hook to the end of the line, baiting up, and gently tossing the hooked bait in the chum line behind the boat, and playing out line so the bait will sink and move away from the boat along with the chum. Bigger, bulkier baits such as shedder crab chunks will often spin when floated in a chum slick. It's usually better to bait up with thin, tapered strips of squid, bluefish and spot, which will flutter enticingly in the moving water. In a strong current, a small rubber-core sinker may be needed to help get the bait down in the fast-moving water. Chum lines also attract small baitfish. Casting and retrieving artificials that resemble small baitfish—including bucktails, leadheads with plastics, plugs, spoons and jigs—is often a very effective tactic on weaks and specks as they cruise chum slicks.

Current is critical when it comes to chumming. A moderate current will effectively disburse chum great distances while it steadily sinks toward the bottom. This creates a comprehensive slick from the surface of the water to bottom that covers a rather vast area, and it will attract fish from far and wide. On the other hand, when there's very little or no water movement, the chum won't go anywhere, or may just slowly sink to the bottom very near the boat.

Another problem altogether is a strong current which will quickly carry the chum long distances from the boat before it can sink much below the surface. This is ineffective because the chum stays high in the water column, usually well above bottom-hugging weakfish and speckled trout. It only begins to sink in the strong current after it's too far away from the boat to be of much benefit to the anglers. When chumming in a strong current, or in deep water, it's often a good idea to lower the chum bucket or bag from the boat to the bottom. As the chum comes out of the bucket or bag it's already near the bottom where the fish are. One way to do this is to weigh down the chum bucket or bag with one or more bricks or rocks. Or an onion bag or some other type of mesh bag containing chum can be tied to the anchor line, just above the anchor, before the anchor is dropped over.

Drag And Grab A Wreck Or Reef

A popular anchor among wreck fishermen is one made from the metal bars used to reinforce concrete, commonly referred to as "rebar". Four pieces of rebar stick out from the anchor shaft and are bent into the shapes of hooks.

Position the boat upcurrent from the wreck, toss the anchor over and allow the drifting boat to pull the anchor along the bottom. Hopefully, the anchor will be dragged right into the wreck where the rebar hooks will grab and hold. Then shorten up on the anchor rope as much as possible until the boat sits right on top of the structure. This enables bait fishermen and jiggers to fish straight up and down on the fish-holding structure.

At the end of the day the anchor may have a stubborn grip on the wreck and tugging on the rope just won't loosen it; try slowly moving the boat directly over and past the anchor while keeping a taut line –the rebar will straighten out some, freeing the anchor from the wreck. The rebar is flexible enough to be easily bent back into shape.

Another wreck anchoring technique involves locating and marking the wreck with a marker buoy, and then motoring directly upcurrent from the buoy. The anchor, usually a Danforth anchor, is then dropped, and the boat is allowed to drift back until it reaches the marker buoy. After checking that the anchor has a good bite on the bottom, the anchor line is tied to a cleat and the boat is secured over the wreck. If, after motoring upcurrent of the wreck and dropping the anchor, the boat does not come near the buoy when it drifts back, then it will be necessary to pull the anchor and try again. This takes time and requires considerable effort, but remember, the fish are on the wreck and it's imperative that baits and lures be fished directly on the structure.

Some anglers will mark the wreck with a buoy, then they motor upcurrent and drop the anchor, but they will tie off and position the boat while it is still upcurrent of the buoy which is marking the wreck.

They then either cast toward the buoy suspended over the wreck, or drop down their bait or lure and allow the current to push it back toward the structure. Other anglers position their anchored boat slightly off to one side of the wreck and they will fish the structure by casting lures and baits to it.

Baits commonly used to catch weaks on wrecks include squid and clam strips, sand fleas and chunks of shedder crab. Tog, sea bass and stripers also inhabit wrecks and they'll gobble down those same baits and will at times bring some unexpected variety to the weakfish catch. A simple bottom rig is recommended. In a two to three-foot piece of 50 to 60-pound leader, tie a surgeon's end loop at the bottom of the leader to hold the sinker. Just above that, tie a dropper loop and slip a 3/0 to 5/0 hook over that loop. A second dropper loop, to hold a second hook, can be tied a short distance above the first dropper loop. I prefer to fish only one hook at a time on wrecks in order to reduce the number of snags.

Bucktails, leadheads with plastic tails, spoons and jigs will also trigger weakfish strikes when fished on and over wrecks. Be sure to bring an extensive selection of hooks, sinkers and lures as many snags and lost tackle can be expected when probing wrecks for big weakfish. Leaving lots of tackle on the wrecks can get frustrating

A GPS or loran, a color scope or LCD fishfinder and a chart will help you pin-point good inshore wrecks.

and a bit costly at times, and frequently tying on new rigs and lures cuts into valuable fishing time. Yet it's all part of the wreck fishing game, and it also makes a successful day of wreck fishing all the more rewarding and satisfying.

Trolling

There seems to be little middle ground when it comes to trolling. Either you like it, or you don't. Those who like it get a great deal of enjoyment out of trolling and spend a considerable amount of time pulling bucktails, plugs, spoons and plastic baits for weakfish, speckled trout and all of their favorite species. At the other end of the spectrum are anglers for whom trolling is out of the question. They would much rather cast and retrieve lures and flies, or bounce bait and jigs on the bottom. They consider trolling nothing more than an extended boat ride. They feel much of the sport and excitement of battling fish are lost when fish are winched in on heavy trolling tackle. No matter which side of the issue you come down on, there is no denying that trolling catches a lot of weaks and specks, and is especially productive on big trophy fish. Because trolling can very effectively locate and catch fish, every serious weakfish and speckled trout angler owes it to himself to develop an understanding of how

Trollers use wire line to get bucktails and other artificials down deep and on the bottom where many of the biggest weakfish and speckled trout are most often caught.

and where to successfully troll for trout.

Even fishermen who don't like to troll can use it to pinpoint concentrations of fish, and then they can break out the casting or bottom bouncing tackle and have fun catching them. Trolling covers more water more quickly than drifting, and it can be used to eliminate a lot of unproductive water. Once a fish or two is taken while trolling, the boat can be anchored or drifted in that specific area, enabling the fishermen to concentrate their efforts on a location that is known to hold fish.

My friend Pete Dressler compares the bottom of the bay or ocean with a football field. A football field is 100 yards long, yet during a game the players aren't distributed evenly over the entire field. Instead, they're concentrated around the football. If the ball is at the 20 yard line and the teams are at the line of scrimmage, most of the 22 players on the field will be on or very near the 20 yard line, while the rest of the field–a majority of the field–will be empty. The same is true of the bottom of the bay or ocean. Fish don't spread out evenly over the bottom, instead, they gather in certain spots. Even when fishing shoals, sloughs and channel edges, the fish usually are not found all over the structure, but rather in bunches in specific locations on the structure. Trolling enables you to quickly cover a great deal of bottom and search out the spots that hold fish. Then the choice is yours whether to troll, anchor or drift on those concentrations of fish.

Big weakfish and speckled trout do much of their feeding directly on the bottom. That's where they root up crabs, shrimp and much of the other food that sustains them. Trollers get their lures and baits on the bottom by using superbraided lines and wire line that cut through the water much better than monofilament. Their trolling rigs also feature heavy sinkers. Bouncing a sinker along the bottom while trolling ensures that the lure or bait is constantly on the bottom and in the fish strike zone. In other types of fishing, such as casting and retrieving, the bait spends a great deal of the time up and off the bottom, and even out of the water, in areas where the fish can't see the bait or grab it.

Some anglers favor downriggers which enable them to troll deep with light tackle that doesn't include wire or superbraided lines, or heavy sinkers or planers. The fishing line has only the lure tied to the end of it. About 50 to 75 feet ahead of the lure, the line from the reel is slipped into a clip at the downrigger weight. The downrigger weight is on a cable and can be lowered, along with the clip holding the line, to exactly the desired depth (very near the bottom). The lure is pulled through the water behind the downrigger weight - weakfish and speckled trout anglers should allow at least the above-mentioned 50 to 75 feet of line between the downrigger weight and the lure. When a fish strikes the lure the line will pull free from the clip, enabling the angler to fight the fish on light tackle

SHALLOW-WATER TROLLING RIG

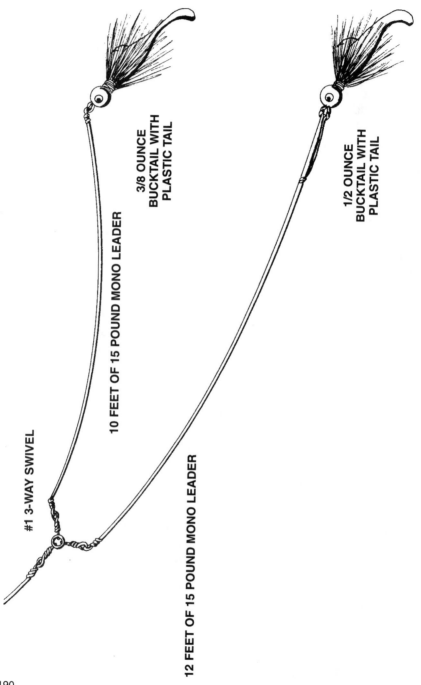

3/8 OUNCE BUCKTAIL WITH PLASTIC TAIL

1/2 OUNCE BUCKTAIL WITH PLASTIC TAIL

10 FEET OF 15 POUND MONO LEADER

12 FEET OF 15 POUND MONO LEADER

#1 3-WAY SWIVEL

OPEN-WATER, DOUBLE-BUCKTAIL TROLLING RIG

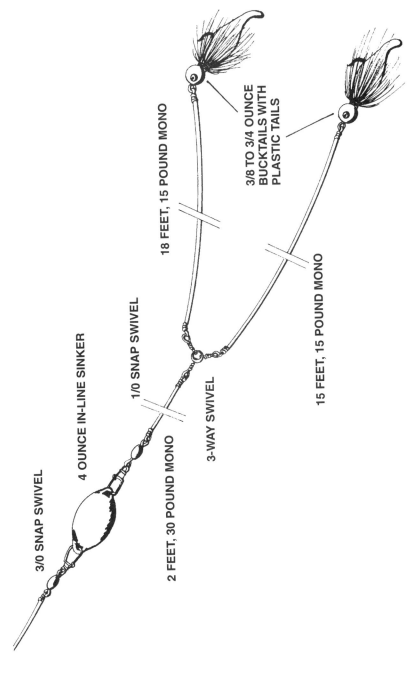

3/8 TO 3/4 OUNCE BUCKTAILS WITH PLASTIC TAILS

18 FEET, 15 POUND MONO

15 FEET, 15 POUND MONO

1/0 SNAP SWIVEL

3-WAY SWIVEL

4 OUNCE IN-LINE SINKER

2 FEET, 30 POUND MONO

3/0 SNAP SWIVEL

DOUBLE-BUCKTAIL TROLLING RIG

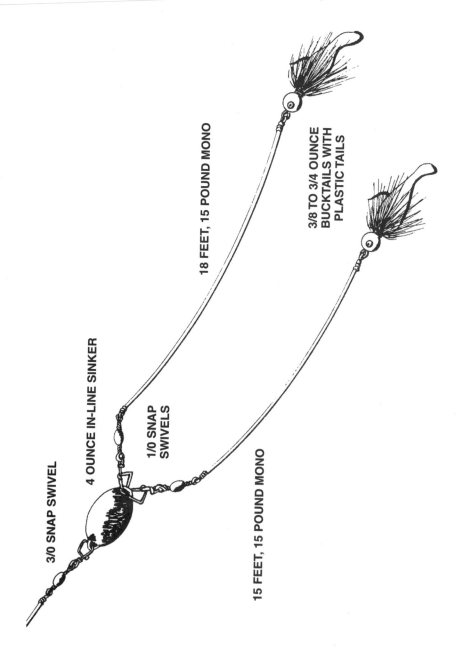

18 FEET, 15 POUND MONO

3/8 TO 3/4 OUNCE BUCKTAILS WITH PLASTIC TAILS

4 OUNCE IN-LINE SINKER

1/0 SNAP SWIVELS

3/0 SNAP SWIVEL

15 FEET, 15 POUND MONO

WIRE LINE OR SUPERBRAID TROLLING RIG

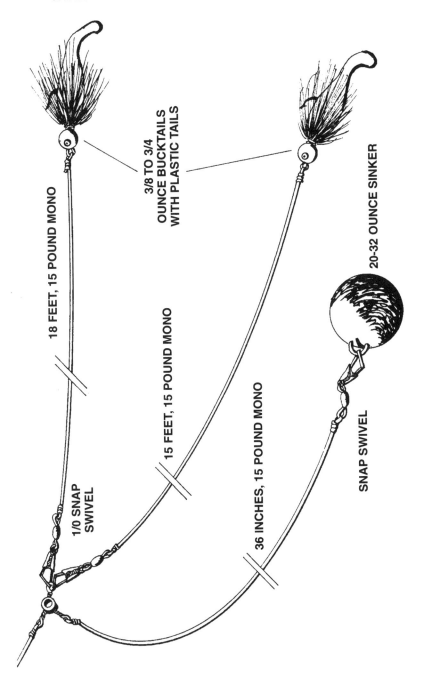

3/8 TO 3/4 OUNCE BUCKTAILS WITH PLASTIC TAILS

18 FEET, 15 POUND MONO

15 FEET, 15 POUND MONO

36 INCHES, 15 POUND MONO

20-32 OUNCE SINKER

SNAP SWIVEL

1/0 SNAP SWIVEL

while someone else retrieves the cable and downrigger weight. The downrigger weight and cable are lowered and retrieved by a pulley that is mounted in the stern of the boat; it also features a counter that indicates how much cable has been let out (how deep the downrigger weight and lure are). Bucktails, parachutes and plugs (such as Mann's Stretch 18) are commonly trolled on downriggers for weakfish and speckled trout.

Trolling enables anglers to thoroughly cover structure and present their lures and baits exactly as desired, even on days when the wind and/or current would not allow for effective drifting or anchoring. Weakfish and speckled trout are like striped bass in that they prefer to ambush their meals, in comparison to speedy bluefish and Spanish mackerel that often chase down other fish. Big weaks and specks are especially wary and often less aggressive and they lay low in search of easy meals. So when it comes to trolling speed, slow is good, and slower is better. It's all but impossible to troll too slowly for weaks and specks. To slow the boat as much as possible, some anglers troll into the current and into the wind.

Back bays and other shallow-water areas can also be trolled in an attempt to locate fish. Small bucktails, parachutes, spoons and plugs

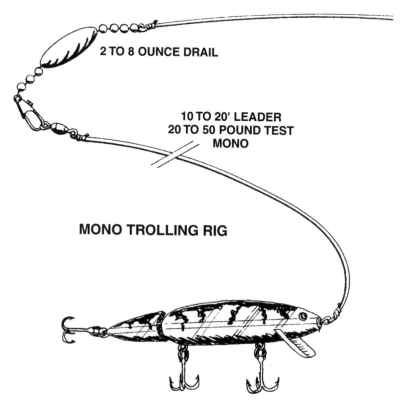

2 TO 8 OUNCE DRAIL

10 TO 20' LEADER
20 TO 50 POUND TEST
MONO

MONO TROLLING RIG

are trolled on monofilament line, and usually without sinkers, as there is no need to fish deep. A slow and quiet presentation works best for weaks and specks in shallow water, which makes an electric motor perfect for this type of trolling.

Party Boat Weakfish

The seas were calm and the sunset glorious. It was a perfect August evening for fishing as the mates aboard the head boat Starlight out of Wildwood, New Jersey, dropped anchor and began slinging chum. Following the mates' instructions, we baited our bottom rigs by hooking one or two whole dead butterfish through the eyes. It was relatively quiet along the rails as we allowed our baits to sink to the bottom, each angler enjoying the fading daylight and anticipating in their own way the exciting and hard-fighting bluefish action they hoped would soon erupt. "I've got one!" cried an angler as he battled a strong and stubborn fish. Then several other anglers hooked up. Finally, the confrontation between the first fisherman and his quarry approached its zenith as the fish neared the surface. Flashing in the day's last rays of sunlight and in the boat's lights shining down from above, the hooked fish seemed to blast a charge of electricity through all of the anglers as we glimpsed what we had originally assumed was a big bluefish. Instead, it was an 8 to 10-pound weakfish that was being lead to the gaff!

Incredibly, to everyone's absolute astonishment, the water around the boat was suddenly alive with fish as thousands of additional big weakfish had followed the first hooked fish to the surface. Anglers frantically reeled up their butterfish baits and dangled them on the surface where several weakfish would simultaneously attack and one would be hooked! It quickly became clear to us that these immense weakfish were in no hurry to sound, and some anglers quickly replaced their bottom rigs with bucktails, surgical tube eels, and other artificials. Casting wasn't necessary as the only requirement was to drop a lure or bait straight down into the water where it would instantly be charged by several hungry weakfish. It was literally non-stop action for everyone on board. Soon coolers and fish bags were bulging and the deck was covered knee-deep in flopping weakfish, so we started tossing fish into the cabin—usually a definite no-no on most head boats. But this was different. The sweat-soaked, arm-weary anglers who continued to hook and battle 8 to 12-pound weakfish one-after-another had never witnessed or enjoyed fabulous fishing like this before.

The fish stayed on the surface, in the chum slick and in the boat's lights, and the mayhem continued for hours. Shortly after midnight, the yells and screams from delighted anglers had dwindled considerably. Many fishermen had actually walked away from the excitement and, wherever they could find room among the huge piles of weakfish, they sat down to cool off with a cold drink. Yet there were still so many weakfish on the surface that it was impossible to tell that a single fish had been removed from the vast school.

I enjoyed that incredible-but-true fishing adventure in the early 1980s, during the weakfish wonder years. It was not a once-in-a-lifetime occurrence, as other New Jersey and Delaware head boats reported occasional similar weakfish eruptions during the late 70s and early 80s. While nearly two decades have passed since the last of that awesome action, head boats have continued to produce good weakfish catches for anglers all along the Atlantic Coast.

A key to fishing on head boats, especially when there is a crowd on board, is for all anglers to fish in the same way, with the same type of tackle, as much as possible. Anyone who deviates from the standard approach will probably tangle lines and jangle the nerves of his fellow fishermen. In other words, if everyone is bottom fishing with cut bait, then an angler who would instead cast and retrieve a bucktail is likely to fall out of favor very quickly.

Common weakfish tactics on party boats include bottom fishing with one-hook and two-hook store-bought and homemade rigs baited with squid strips and/or pieces of shedder crab and weighted with 4 to 8-ounce sinkers. Fishing artificial lures on head boats for

Anglers looking to increase their success on party boats should bring along baits such as peeler crab, bloodworms or cut bait in addition to the squid strips normally supplied on the boat.

weakfish usually involves bottom jigging with bucktails or plain leadhead jigs with a plastic worm and/or squid strip, Hopkins Shorty spoons, Stingsilvers, and Crippled Herring jigs. Usually, there is no casting involved as anglers simply belly-up to the rail and drop their bait rigs or jigging lures straight to the bottom. Spinning tackle, and conventional or baitcasting outfits, with 12 to 20-pound test line, can both be used. Yet many experienced party boat sharpies say an outfit featuring a revolving-spool reel enables the angler to better control the line and better detect strikes than does spinning tackle.

While it is important for everyone on a head boat to fish in the same manner, there are steps that individual anglers can take to improve their odds. When it comes to bait for bottom rigs and jigs, most party boats provide squid strips. A day or two before a party boat trip, savvy anglers will also purchase or obtain other fresh baits to bring with them on the big boat, including live shedder (peeler) crabs, bloodworms, grass shrimp, and fresh cut bluefish and spot. It may be necessary to lug on the boat an extra cooler containing these baits, but believe me it is worth it to bring these baits and to keep them cool and fresh. If a bluefish, spot, croaker or sea robin is caught while fishing for weakfish, the angler can quickly produce a supply of fresh bait by using a fillet knife to cut those fish into strip baits. These extra fresh baits will often produce much better than head boat-issued squid, and the extra effort and expense of obtaining them may very well transform what would have been an ordinary day on the water into a super-productive party boat trip that won't soon be forgotten.

Chapter Nine

THE END GAME

There's a strike! All of your senses go on full alert - you're instantly energized as the moment of truth has suddenly arrived. This is exactly what you have planned for and prepared for, and now it's "make or break" time. This split second, and the next few upcoming minutes are absolutely crucial, and your decisions and actions will determine the outcome. Stay relatively calm, think clearly, do the right things at the proper times - and throw in a little luck for good measure - and you will achieve your ultimate goal of catching a fish. On the other hand…well, let's think positive and not go there.

For most anglers, myself included, a boat ride or day on the beach is nice, but it's less than complete unless fish are caught. There's a lot of satisfaction that comes with understanding and locating your quarry and deceiving it into attempting to eat a lure or bait you have presented. But getting strikes is one thing, total reward comes when fish are hooked, battled, and boated or beached.

This final chapter is all about some very important aspects of fishing. It contains information on how, and when to properly set the hook, if the hook even needs to be set at all. Playing the fish - perhaps the single most enjoyable experience in all of fishing - is also discussed in this chapter. We'll also look at netting and landing fish, safely handling and unhooking fish so they'll be healthy and more likely to survive when released, tagging fish, and how to turn your weakfish and speckled trout catches into scrumptious meals.

Setting The Drag

First things first. Before getting in knock-down drag-out fights with big hooked weakfish and speckled trout, before setting the hook, and actually before making the first cast, it's crucial to make sure the reel's drag is set correctly. The general rule is that the drag should be set at about 25 percent of the line's pound test rating. In other words, with 12-pound test line, the drag should give line when three pounds of pressure is applied to the line. With 15-pound test, the drag should be set at just under four pounds. With 17-pound test, a drag setting of about 4-1/4 pounds is recommended. A drag setting of about five pounds is the general rule for 20-pound test.

Many fishermen set their drags by feel - they use their hand to pull line against the drag and loosen or tighten the drag until it gives line at what seems like a reasonable amount of pressure. However, fishermen who do this almost always end up with a drag setting that far exceeds the rule of 25 percent of the line's pound test rating. The most accurate form of setting the drag involves tying the end of the line from the reel to a hand scale, and then pulling the hand scale until line comes off the reel. The scale will plainly indicate how many pounds of pressure are being applied to the line when the drag gives line.

To many anglers, a drag setting of 25 percent of the line's pound test rating will seem extremely light. But a lightly-set drag is obviously much more forgiving than a drag that's set too tightly. It's better to temporarily lose a little line off the reel than to have the line snap when a strong fish makes a sudden run against a tight drag.

Setting The Hook

Weakfish and speckled trout strikes can range from arm-jolting blasts to a single, subtle tap. It depends on any number of factors, including the type of tackle, bait or lure being used, water temperature, and the size of the fish. There are even times when the angler will feel nothing, when just a slight twitch or barely-detectable movement in the line where it meets the water will be on the only indication that a fish has shown interest in the offering.

Superbraided lines, and some new low-stretch super-sensitive monofilament lines, enable anglers to detect even the softest of strikes. That makes them popular among weakfish and speckled trout anglers fishing bait on bottom rigs, and also casting plugs and bucktails, and bottom jigging with metals. However, I believe these characteristics are a detriment when livelining and in other applications where a drop-back may be necessary, as the highly-sensitive line provides precious little time for a drop-back before the fish detects resistance and spits out the bait. In these situations I prefer monofilament as it will stretch and isn't as sensitive, giving me more time to react and drop back before setting the hook.

When fishing bait, bucktailing, plugging and jigging, most anglers respond to a strike with an immediate hookset. Some may pause for just an instant, and even lower the rod tip to provide additional line so the fish can get the lure or bait farther into its mouth, before setting

In most fishing situations involving monofilament, setting the hook involves making sure there is no slack in the line, then rapidly and firmly raising the rod tip to drive the hook into the fish's jaw.

the hook, but the majority of anglers strike the moment a fish is felt on the line. Because it will stretch, sometimes as much as 15 percent, monofilament requires a harder, more vigorous hookset than does superbraided lines. Only a slight hookset is needed with super-braided lines, and some anglers don't even set the hook at all, they just start reeling when they get a bite. A hard hookset with no-stretch superbraided lines may quickly snatch the bait or lure away from the fish, or may actually rip it out of the tissue of the fish's jaw and mouth. Driving the hook into a fish hard with these unforgiving lines can cause a sharp impact very capable of shattering a graphite rod. With both monofilament and superbraided lines, it's very important to take out any slack before setting the hook. This allows the upward movement of the rod to quickly drive the hook into the fish's jaw.

When livelining, resist the urge to strike the instant there's a pickup. Instead, it's important to give line to prevent the fish from detecting resistance from the angler. Livelining requires a drop-back, as the fish will need some time to get the bait fully into its mouth. Baitcasting or conventional reels are recommended, as the spool can be kept disengaged and the angler only has to lift their thumb from the spool to give line the moment a pickup is detected. After the fish has had the bait for at least a good five-count, the angler then engages the spool, takes up all slack, and sets the hook firmly (with monofilament) to make sure the hook has been sufficiently embedded in the fish.

Playing And Landing Fish

Now comes perhaps the most enjoyable and challenging time of all - the fish is hooked and the battle has begun. The size of the fish, the type of tackle being used, and water temperature will primarily determine just how rugged the battle will be.

The rod is the key component in subduing fish. Keep the rod tip held high and a hooked fish will never have a moment's rest. The rod will constantly apply pressure and tire the fish struggling against the rod's pressure. The rod will also absorb much of the shock and pressure that are applied when a strong fish takes off on a sudden run or violently shakes its head. The reel's drag also comes into play. When set properly, it will give line to prevent the line from breaking under the pressure being applied by the fish. Some anglers get excited or nervous as line comes off the reel and will attempt to stop it by pressing down with their thumb on the spool of baitcasting or conventional reels, or by pressing against the edge of the spool on a spinning reel. This is often a mistake as a little too much pressure

Success! A big weakfish has been hooked, battled, netted and is about to be boated.

can cause the line to snap. The drag plays a crucial role in battles with hooked fish. In fact, the bigger the fish and/or the lighter the tackle, the more important the drag. Give your drags the care and attention they deserve, set them properly, and then allow them to do their very important job. And do not attempt to reel in line with a spinning reel as the drag is giving line, as this will cause line twist.

The rod should be held fairly steady when slugging it out with hooked fish. It's not necessary to do a lot of rod pumping. Just hold the rod steady and reel. Raising the rod tip, and then lowering it while line is reeled in, may create slack in the line, if only for an instant. But that very brief moment of loose line may be all that's needed for the fish to get off. Constantly raising and lowering the rod tip can also cause the hook to wear a hole in the fish's mouth, and the hook may slip out through this hole. This is especially true when fishing with no-stretch superbraided line and when battling weakfish –the "weak" in weakfish comes from the soft tissue in their mouth which can be easily torn.

As the amount of line between the rod tip and the fish diminishes, so does the room for angler error. Every miscue is magnified as a hooked fish is brought closer and closer to the boat, beach, bridge, jetty or pier. The fish may be oh-so-close and in sight, but it's not over yet. Don't get complacent, or anxious, to the point where a careless mistake could be made. Stay calm and be patient as the fight appears to be drawing to an end.

Even a fish lying over on its side on the surface and seemingly near exhaustion may summon the strength to make one last run for freedom. Never tighten the drag at this point, and do not attempt to slow or stop the drag with your thumb, fingers or hand. When there is little line between the rod tip and fish, the less the line can stretch and the less shock it can absorb. A suddenly-surging fish can easily impact the line enough to break it–a smooth and properly-working drag will save the day in this scenario.

It's also important to keep the fish on a taut line. As the angler or a companion prepare to net or beach the fish, the rod tip should be held high and kept there, so the rod maintains steady pressure on the fish. If the rod tip is allowed to dip, even if only briefly, it may create enough slack in the line to allow the fish to come off. Or, detecting that the pressure against it has stopped, the fish may make a dash for it, and the charging fish could very well snap the line as it pulls out all of the slack and suddenly jerks against the tight line.

In the 1970s and 1980s, many big tiderunners were gaffed. But no more. Many states now have laws that prohibit gaffing any fish that are subject to minimum size limits, even if the fish are obviously well over the minimum size limit. In this age of conservation, when great numbers of anglers diligently protect our marine resources by

If at all possible, do not touch a fish that is to be released, as handling a fish can remove its protective layer of slime.

releasing many of the fish they catch, regardless of size, it just makes no sense to gaff any weakfish or speckled trout. Some jetty anglers will use a small gaff, usually fashioned from a large hook that would normally be used to catch tuna or sharks, to carefully lip-gaff weakfish or speckled trout that are so large that they can't be lifted onto the rocks without fear of the line breaking or waves pounding the fish against the boulders. Carefully handled, these lip-gaffed fish can be released without serious injury.

When netting a fish, make sure the net is untangled and ready to go, and has not snagged any hooks, lures or other items that could cause damage to a fish in the net. Frabill and other companies now market "hook proof" and "spook proof" nets, and also knotless nets, and nets that have been specially treated so as not to damage the scales or rub off the protective slime on fish. Never put a net in the water behind a fish. The fish may sense the presence of the net and bolt forward, away from the net, and perhaps break the line. Always place the net in the water in front of the fish. That way, if the fish is spooked it will dart directly into the net, not away from it.

Since coming into contact with a net can potentially harm a fish, it's a good idea to leave small fish and other fish to be released in the water while they're unhooked. Or grab the leader and lift the fish out of the water without using a net. Never handle a fish with dry hands; either hold it with a wet rag or wet your hands before touching the fish. Carefully subdue the fish as much as possible so it doesn't injure itself by flopping and thrashing around. A good way to do that is to place a wet rag over its head and eyes. Holding fish upside down also seems to quiet them.

Gently remove the hook if at all possible. Only on the deepest-hooked fish should the leader be cut and the fish released with the hook still in it. A pair of needle-nose pliers, or any one of a number of de-hooker devices that are specially designed to free even hooks lodged deep in a fish's throat, can be used to remove a hook without inflicting any more damage than is absolutely necessary. If photographs are to be taken, snap them quickly. It's very important to keep the fish out of the water as briefly as possible.

Small fish, which are usually overpowered by the tackle they are caught on, are very often fresh and energetic and will rapidly swim off the moment they hit the water. Other fish may need to be revived. With wet hands, while supporting the fish under its head and near the tail, place it back in the water with its head facing into the current so water enters the fish's mouth and flows back over its gills. Slowly and patiently move the fish back and forth in the water until it's revived and swims off on its own.

When releasing a weakfish, try to keep it out of the water for the shortest time possible to ensure it swims away strong and healthy.

Fish Tagging

There is so much we don't know about weakfish, speckled trout and all of the predators, baitfish and other life that inhabit our marine waters. Recreational anglers can play a very important role in helping scientists and fisheries managers learn more about weakfish and speckled trout by tagging the fish they release. Before tagging fish to be released, anglers should write on the tags all of the information that is requested, which usually includes the date and location of the catch, and the size of the fish at the time it was caught. It's also important that anglers call the phone numbers on the tags of any tagged fish they happen to catch, or mail the tags and requested information to the address provided on the tag. When recaptured and reported by fishermen, scientists gain great insight into the migration patterns, spawning activities, preferred habitats, growth characteristics and abundance of these fish. This information can be used by fisheries managers to implement weakfish and speckled trout regulations that are fair to fishermen while at the same time very protective of the resource to ensure that we and our children will have plenty of great fishing opportunities to enjoy in the years ahead.

Tagging fish can assist scientists and fisheries managers in learning more about the biological characteristics and habits of game fish like weakfish and speckled trout.

Fish tags and tagging kits can be obtained through a number of sources. One is the American Littoral Society, Sandy Hook, Highlands, New Jersey 07732. To receive tags through the ALS, anglers need to be a member. ALS membership is only $25 for individuals, and $30 for clubs. A tag kit is $6 for a set of 10. Along with weakfish and speckled trout, the tags can be used on other inshore marine game fish, including striped bass, bluefish, summer flounder and winter flounder. For more information, or to receive a fish tagging brochure, call Pam Carlsen at ALS at (732) 291-0055.

FISH Unlimited also conducts a fish-tagging program. It involves a clip-on, monel tag that fastens securely to the dorsal, pectoral or tail fin of any fish. It is applied with a special type of pliers, and when fastened, will stay on the fish for its lifetime. The non-invasive FISH Unlimited Tagging Program tags do not harm any internal organs.

More than 21,000 tags have been issued to anglers around the world who are tagging a wide range of freshwater and saltwater fish, including weakfish and speckled trout. FISH Unlimited Tagging Kits cost only $12 for the applicator, 10 tags and 10 data cards. Refills of the 10 tags and data cards are just $5 afterwards. FISH Unlimited members receive a 20 percent discount. Fishing clubs can purchase 1,000 or more tags (personalized tags) and applicators at a discount.

After a tagged weakfish is re-caught and the tag number reported, a detailed history of the fish is forwarded to the angler who originally released the fish.

When a fish is tagged, and the data card returned to FISH Unlimited's national office, the information is entered into a dedicated database. So far, some 5,000 entries have been entered into the database which will be sent to two universities to be analyzed and put into report form.

When a tagged fish is caught again and the tag number reported, both the original tagger and the angler recatching the fish are sent a detailed history of the fish that describes growth rates, migratory patterns, time at large, and other interesting information. All participants are also sent a FISH Unlimited Tagging Program Pin.

For more information, or to order tags, call FISH Unlimited at 800-621-1964.

Food Value

With proper attention and handling, both weakfish and speckled trout are quite tasty and provide scrumptious meals. As with any fish, after they're pulled from the water, unhooked and quickly admired and photographed, it's important to immediately cool them on ice. Weakies and specks intended for the dinner table shouldn't be flopped into a bucket or bag, or tossed aside so the angler can

To ensure the best-tasting weakfish and speckled trout, fish intended for the dinner table should be placed on ice immediately after capture.

FILLETING YOUR CATCH

1. CUT DOWN TO THE BONE.

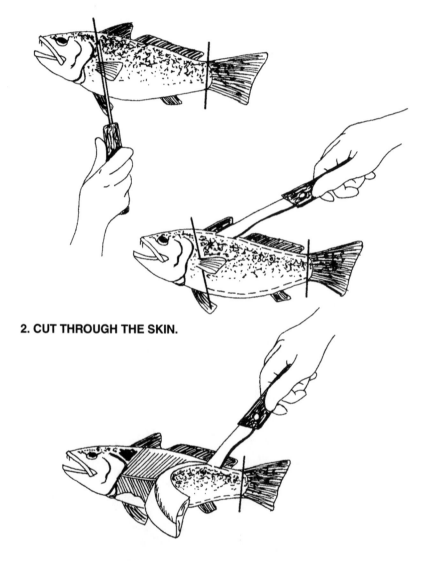

2. CUT THROUGH THE SKIN.

3. SLICE ALONG BACKBONE TO THE TAIL.

QUICK-CLEAN METHOD

quickly get back to catching more fish. Instead, take a few brief moments and make sure fish are properly cared for - the rewards will be well worth it. While fish can be adequately stored and chilled in coolers containing sea water, or bags of ice, or ice blocks, the ideal method of most quickly, thoroughly and evenly chilling fish is to bury them–completely surround them–in crushed ice. With ice bags, blocks and chips, it's a good idea to occasionally drain from the cooler any water that may have accumulated as the ice melts.

Weakfish and speckled trout are most commonly filleted and skinned (some people prefer to scale the fish and leave the skin on the fillets). Or the fish is scaled, gutted and the head is removed, and after cooking the bones can easily be lifted out with a fork. Weakfish and speckled trout are often baked, broiled, fried or smoked, and both the white meat of weakfish and delicate flesh of speckled trout are delicious. Both species are popular items on restaurant menus, and will often appear as "trout" on many seafood restaurant menus. Many people also enjoy meals provided by weakfish roe.

Delicious Recipes

Gary Diamond's Char-Broiled Weakfish

Freshly-caught fish cooked on the grill is absolutely delicious. You need a gas grill and a stainless steel screen for grilling fish (keeps the fillets from falling through the grill). The screens are available in the housewares department of many stores, and through mail-order sporting goods suppliers.

Ingredients:
1 pound skinless weakfish fillets (two servings)
Old Bay Seafood Seasoning
Lite Mayonnaise

Directions:
Fire up the gas grill and set the flame at low to medium heat. Allow the grill to preheat for approximately 10 minutes. While the grill is heating, wash the weakfish fillets in cold water, remove any dark meat and pat dry with a paper towel. Spray the cooking screen with non-stick vegetable oil, place the fillets on the screen, then coat with a quarter-inch layer of mayonnaise. Sprinkle with Old Bay Seafood Seasoning, place on the grill and close the cover. Grill approximately 5 to 10 minutes or until the meat easily flakes. Serve hot with a side dish of steamed broccoli covered with cheese sauce and twice baked potatoes. Incredible!

Tom Pagliaroli's Quick 'n Spicy Weaks

Directions:

Arrange 1-1/2 to 2 pounds of weakfish fillets on a well-buttered (lightly-salted butter) shallow baking dish.

Combine 2-1/2 tablespoons of soy sauce, two tablespoons of olive oil, 1-1/2 tablespoons of fresh (or MinuteMaid) lemon juice, 1-1/2 tablespoons of Worcestershire sauce, 3/4 teaspoon of chili powder and 1/4 teaspoon of garlic powder.

Splash in a few shakes of Tabasco sauce. Mix well and pour over the fillets.

Broil 12 to 14 minutes, testing with a fork until the flesh flakes easily. A three bean salad, crusty French bread, chilled blush wine and coconut custard pie complete the piscine masterpiece.

Gary Diamond's Smoked Weakfish

Brine Solution:

2 quarts cold water
1/2 cup Kosher salt
1 cup dark brown sugar
4 tablespoons Old Bay Seafood Seasoning
4 tablespoons onion bits
1/2 teaspoon garlic powder
1 tablespoon lemon juice
6 drops Worcestershire sauce

Directions:

Mix brine solution thoroughly until salt and sugar are completely dissolved. Skin and fillet fish, remove all dark meat along the lateral line, then rinse fillets in cold water and cut into serving-size segments. Using a plastic container with lid, pour in a small amount of brine (approximately 1/2-inch deep), then add a layer of fillets. Add sufficient brine to completely cover fillets. Repeat the process by alternately adding fillets and brine until all fillets are completely immersed in brine solution. Seal the container with a lid or plastic wrap and refrigerate for three to four days. Rock the container at least twice daily to prevent settling.

With the proper gear and knowledge of their quarry, fishermen up and down the coast can get in on the exciting fishing opportunities provided by weakfish and speckled trout.

Cooking & Smoking:

Using a broiler pan sprayed liberally with non-stick cooking oil, bake the fillets in a 350-degree, preheated over for 20 minutes (25 minutes for thicker fillets) or until the meat easily flakes. While the fish bakes, spray the smoker racks with vegetable oil and fill the smoker pan level with hickory, cherry or alder chips. After baking, place the fillets on the smoker racks, plug in the smoker and smoke for one to three hours or until the fillets are golden brown. Another pan of fresh chips may be added about halfway through the process for additional, smoky flavor. Refrigerate overnight in Zip-Loc bags before eating.

Hi-C's Fish Cakes

Tom Pagliaroli provides this delicious recipe, via his friend "Hi-C", whose freezer Tom says is never occupied by anything he didn't catch or otherwise subdue. Here is one of his favorite uses for frozen fillets.

Directions:

Arrange 2 pounds of weakfish fillets in a broiling pan that is first sprayed with PAM (butter or olive oil flavored).

Sprinkle fillets with two, 2-1/2 tablespoons of Old Bay seasoning and broil until fillets are lightly browned, turning once. Place fillets in a deep bowl and mash.

Add three tablespoons of soy sauce, one tablespoon of spicy mustard, one-half cup of seasoned (herb, country, Italian) bread crumbs, two eggs and one-half teaspoon each of salt and black pepper. Mix well.

Form one 1/4-pound "hamburger-sized" patty and then coat both sides with seasoned bread crumbs.

Heat 1/4-inch to 1/2-inch vegetable oil in a deep frying pan until almost smoking, and then carefully add the cakes.

Serve with cole slaw, French (or steak) fries, an ice-cold beverage of choice, and follow with rice pudding for dessert.

ABOUT THE AUTHOR

Keith Kaufman has been fishing since his boyhood days and eventually made the switch from "doing it for fun" to earning a living from sport fishing as Managing Editor of *The Fisherman* magazine's Mid Atlantic Edition from 1989 to 1999. Currently Chief of Community Relations for the Delaware Department of Transportation, Keith remains actively involved with *The Fisherman* as a field editor, frequent contributor, and seminar speaker. He also writes for *Game and Fish* magazine and other outdoor publications. His extensive communications and news journalism experience includes a stint as copywriter for Bass Pro Shops and Offshore Angler catalogs in Springfield, Missouri.

Keith, his wife Stephanie and sons Cody and Ross live near Dover, Delaware. They fish mostly on Delaware Bay, yet each season Keith also spends a considerable amount of time pursuing his favorite species in Chesapeake Bay, and on the inshore grounds off the Delaware, Maryland and Virginia Coast. One of his favorite fishing travel destinations is Sarasota, Florida, and the opportunities it provides for tarpon, snook, redfish and speckled trout.

Keith is a member of the Maryland Saltwater Sportfishermen's Association, Delaware Mobile Sportfishermen, Eastern Shore Anglers Club of Virginia, and Outdoors Writers Association of America. He graduated with honors with a Bachelor of Arts in Communications from East Stroudsburg University in Pennsylvania, and was the recipient of the 1998-1999 Mid-Atlantic Conservation Media Award from the Coastal Conservation Association, Virginia Chapter.

NOTES

NOTES